An Unofficial Roy Fisher

Frontispiece by Ronald King.

A Unofficial Roy Fisher

edited by

Peter Robinson

Shearsman Books
Exeter

First published in the United Kingdom in 2010 by
Shearsman Books Ltd
58 Velwell Road
Exeter EX4 4LD

ISBN 978-1-84861-120-7
First Edition

Copyright original works © Roy Fisher 2010
Copyright editorial matter © Peter Robinson 2010
Copyright bibliographical matter © Derek Slade 2010
Copyright other original poems, prose, and artworks
© individual contributors 2010

Frontispiece copyright © Ronald King 2010
Cover illustration copyright © Ian Tyson 2010

The right of Peter Robinson to be identified as the editor of this work has been asserted by him in accordance with the Copyrights, Designs and Patents Act of 1988.
All rights reserved.

preface

An Unofficial Roy Fisher is an informal gathering of writings that celebrate the art and influence of a unique British poet on the occasion of his eightieth birthday, published as a *festschrift* to that end on 11 June 2010. Fisher himself wrote in 'Style', a poem dedicated to the late Michael Hamburger, that 'my friend Michael … knows good Englishes' and 'knows the language / language gets my poems out of.' In the spirit of 'Style', *An Unofficial Roy Fisher* borrows its title from a volume of Hamburger's translations published by Anvil Press in 1981, a book called *An Unofficial Rilke: Poems 1912 to 1926*. It crossed my mind that if you substitute the name of my favourite living poet for the author of the *Neue Gedichte*, you would get an assonantal chime, an unofficial Fisher. I knew from Derek Slade's Bibliography and an essay by James Keery in *The Thing About Roy Fisher: Critical Studies* (2000) that there exists a fair amount of uncollected poetry, and thought to ask the subject of this collection if he would be willing to allow some of this work to be brought back into print. Roy and I had talked about what would be the organization and contents of his *The Long and the Short of It: Poems 1955–2005*, so I was aware that these uncollected works could not be absorbed into the official oeuvre. Perhaps they might be allowed to see the light of day in *An Unofficial Fisher*? It turned out that they, or some of them at least, could so emerge. First and foremost, then, I must thank Roy Fisher for his collaboration in the editing of this book's first section, a gathering of twenty-one pieces from all stages of his writing life. It struck me that 'unofficial' was a word very much in the spirit of his stance to the world. The book's title contains a number of implications, and I very much suspect that they have relevance to his writings.

An Unofficial Roy Fisher begins, thus, with a gathering of poems and prose pieces by its subject. This is followed by a poet's poets' anthology of new poems by Fisher's extensive international following among significant contemporaries and juniors. Some of them, Fleur Adcock's for instance, take the form of birthday tributes. Others refer or allude to aspects of Roy Fisher's work or personal example that have influenced the poet's poet in question. All the work in this section contributes to that invaluable form of cultural continuity functioning at a level deeper than the current obsession with celebrity status, namely the indelible marks of a style taken to heart by others that has then informed later writing. Led off by a review-like piece on styles of jazz piano by its subject, the Fisher Syndrome Explained is a group of informal essays, articles, reviews, memoirs, and other prose comments on working with Fisher or Fisher's work. Finally, Derek Slade, the poet's bibliographer, provides a memoir of his researches and a checklist covering the decade since the most recent version of his invaluable guide, published in *The Thing about Roy Fisher: Critical Studies*, edited by John Kerrigan and myself a decade ago. All in all, as well as celebrating the eightieth birthday of an invaluable friend and mentor this new collection of work aims to provide a sequence of intriguing insights into the oeuvre and abiding significance of a distinctive literary artist, one whom Edwin Morgan has described, Japanese-fashion, as 'a living national treasure.'

What I like about Roy Fisher's work and his approach to the field of poetry is a quality he has himself called 'honest scepticism'. The poem 'It is Writing', placed after 'For Realism' in *The Long and the Short of It*, pointedly comments on the compulsion to draw a moral from poems. For me, Fisher was the most useful example not only of how a contemporary poet might integrate international influences and local materials, but also how such a writer might embody an ethically inflected view of life so much more by demonstration than assertion. Young writers are forever being advised to 'show' and not 'tell'. Yet, in the most valuable writing, not only is the showing telling, it contains an invaluable outlook to make tell. I recently read Eliot's 1965 Preface to a selection of Edwin Muir's poems, and the idea he lands upon, in the last year of his life, is that Muir had 'integrity' both as a man and in his writing. The sort of thing Eliot wrote of Muir can, I believe, be said for Roy Fisher. He has evolved a way of integrating his intelligence and sensibility in a style that allows him to access his materials and outlook without self-deception or posturing. He has an acute sense of the moment when a style is putting on airs, or gesturing, or is inflated beyond the weight it can lift. I suspect that the poets and writers who have contributed work to *An Unofficial Roy Fisher* will have hoped to approximate as I have, with my own materials and bundles of inner contradiction, to Fisher's sorts of integrity.

I would also like to thank Tony Frazer of Shearsman Books for encouraging and then publishing this retrospect and tribute on the same day that Bloodaxe Books bring out *Standard Midland*, a new collection of Roy Fisher's work, and in the same year that Flood Editions, Chicago, will issue a selection from the poet's oeuvre chosen and introduced by August Kleinzahler. Let me conclude, then, by thanking all the writers and artists who have contributed poetry, prose, and other work to this project—and not least by wishing Roy Fisher a very happy eightieth birthday.

Peter Robinson

contents

an unofficial fisher

A Vision of Four Musicians	10
The Doctor Died	11
Double Morning	13
Heroic Landscape	14
Divisions	15
Night Walkers	16
Script City	17
Something Unmade	18
Results	19
Last Brief Maxims	20
After Midnight	21
The Bachelors Stripped Bare by Their Bride	22
Division of Labour	23
Uncle Jim's Will	24
Big Girl	27
The Discovery of Metre	29
Abraham Darby's Bridge	30
'Dear Gael'	32
'Neighbours, We'll Not Part Tonight!'	33
Art Comes to its Senses Again	35
A Poetry List	36

a poet's poets' anthology

Fleur Adcock	An 80th Birthday Card for Roy	38
Ann Atkinson	Driving Home from Grasmere	39
Eleanor Cooke	Nettle Soup	40
Kelvin Corcoran	The Fisher Piano	42
Peter Didsbury	A Closing Prospect	44
Laurie Duggan	The London Road	46
Peter Hughes	Poly-Olbion	48
Siân Hughes	City	49
August Kleinzahler	Attach to a Place	51
R.F. Langley	Aftermath	52
Angela Leighton	Sheep Count	54
John Matthias	Longs and Shorts	55

Ian McMillan	The Literary Life	57
Peter Middleton	The Walls	58
Michael O'Neill	Never	59
Tom Pickard	the short eared owl as ground nesting metaphor	60
Ralph Pite	*from* walesandbordertrains	61
Ian Pople	A View of Arnhem	64
Richard Price	Jazz Syllabus	66
Tom Raworth	Got On	67
Peter Riley	Bay of Argus	69
Peter Robinson	Unearned Visuals	70
Robert Sheppard	Tentatives	71
Jeffrey Wainwright	The Painter	73
John Welch	Builders	74
David Wheatley	Drypool in Old Photographs	75
John Wilkinson	Trades & Crafts	77

the fisher syndrome explained

Roy Fisher	Death by Adjectives	81
Georgina Hammick	Roy Fisher, letter-writer	85
Charles Lock	A Piece for Roy Fisher	89
Peter Makin	The Hardness of Edges	102
Ralph Pite	Roy Fisher's Waterways	114
Ian Pople	Some observations on 'Experimenting'	128
Richard Price	'Ear-jewels catch a glint': *The Half-Year Letters*	133
Peter Robinson	Collected and Recollected	143
Matthew Sperling	Water	162
Sue Stanford	The Seat of his Pants	170
Jeffrey Wainwright	'Art's Marvellous'	172
David Wheatley	The Secret Laugh of the World	182

a bibliography

Derek Slade	The More He Looked	197
Derek Slade	A Roy Fisher Bibliography 2000–2010	199

Notes on Contributors   217

Roy Fisher

an unofficial fisher

A Vision of Four Musicians

The village will soon forget them, and how they came wandering
As if by chance through the crowd, in clothes the colour of earth;
Stopping unasked, and playing tenuous music
That rose in the heat-haze, suspended, hovering
Fragile as an echo from the journey they came or the path
They had yet to travel; ancient measures, wavering,
Drawn by lean hands from the weathered strings and wood . . .

To see them in fields where the blissful vision
Is undisturbed; pursue that field where the mild heraldic
Creatures sport, free of their myths: the ghostly musician,
Gryphon, and the unicorn—lost his Avenger and Maiden, dissolved
In a friendly sky; to abandon these formulae, learn the hieratic
Art: but here are avenger and maiden, dancing, prepared;
Become them, but offer no victim; never hear music.

Roy Fisher

The Doctor Died

A bad fly bit him. There in the soft hillocks through the olive arch behind his breast, that gold-and-green angular fly from the laughing parrot-woods laid its own chuckle with a jab and a pinch, an acidulous finger for a moment probing his banks; then the coloured poison mounted him, the contented cloud shapes like pink cake, the concealed blood seeping as through wonderful sponge, the leathery towers and bastions of his creamy old youth began to crumble down into white sheets, shooting in folds down his gristly bending skeleton. The cochineal blood runnelled down to his boot-feet, the amber water running afterwards; he stood on dark weights, and the blue phalanges of his fingers did a flick, like fat caterpillars. The falling-down of his back pulled up his head, a rose-coloured, ready-to-cry head in the sunshine. Under the polish of his chin, in mauve caves, blond bristles jerked outwards and outwards, and the bones of his mouth braced themselves and shone. Then what shouts curved out across the mustard-green hillocks, swinging the windmills round and round in the blue over the hilltops! The dusty groundsel grew quicker about his sliding ham-feet, and the clump-trees whistled their gulls home early. The poison danced and beat in the thick shoulders and he groaned in tenor despair; his gold glasses fell off and his blue eyes looked down on his face that shuddered like a cliff. He saw the muscle revolving round his white mouth, and the slow action of his nostrils; he saw the blond hairs start from his cheeks and shrivel into a salad of bleached worms as they reached the air; he saw the oval islands of fat running across beneath the slackening skin of his chest; through the roof of his merely filmed ribs, he saw, far below, the vitreous ocean-basin of his belly, shimmering in furnace colours, and the glowing bread bones of his legs like trees in dark tunnels of fire. Beneath him in the ground were beds of gold and emeralds hammering up at him, many eyes winking and blasting back at his stare.

The sun thrust its muzzle from behind into the rearing mass and shoved it forward a yard onto a red parsley-bush. It melted down through the curved twigs, the skin pricked up across the top, tautening in the afternoon sun like a yellow bag, sagging still as it drained, and with its still-solid pink head staring down among the crimson roots.

Roy Fisher

Double Morning

This long inconstant waking to a day
Hung round with clouds, fouled with dark smears of rain
    On passive walls of grey
That spent-out gusts obscurely trouble,
Makes a contented window, whose wide pane
Looks two ways on a world made double;
Uncertain day, uncertain dream.

I wake under wings, among such wraps
as yield to dawn's murk imperceptibly;
    My limbs succeed to histories that lapse
Slow-fingered into the giant holes of night,
From their persuasions loosing me,
Comforted in this ashen world to remember them:
Dreams of an unknown freedom and appetite.

For I have been through and still am moist from it
Some place of birth in that last untroubled plain of sleep:
    A misted, populous marl-pit
    Where the body's made whole;
And countless human limbs lie folded deep,
Growing in ease under a silvered rain,
In dream-earth's strange and common bowl
Denuded of identity and pain.

Heroic Landscape

A muttering grey sky
           shallow hopeless canopy
Rolled down right to its whitened
Rim around the horizon
                  where the low
Black hills of nightmare start that stretch
To the world's own lip maybe

Here round-limbed long-haired
           women inhabit only
With horses and slow cattle
The staring green-gold pastures
                    among ponds
That glimmer under the winds as they
Feel their way in from the west

And the boy just born
           Sprawling ruddy and fatherless
On the menacing grass where he falls
Laughs out loud at the sky though slime
                      still hears him
And out of him the cord still glistens
Tangled cerulean-silver

Roy Fisher

Divisions

On these exhausted slopes
The snow has lain three days now in clear light,
Mottled on roofs, dragged to roll thick in launders,
In gardens clotted, on clay fields
Spread like a pelt.

Out of the valley floor
Close by a ramp where hoppers lurch
The red-lead girders of a half-built factory
Jut under sketched white lines
Ominous and bare.

And on the hill behind
The snow-scarves tear on red clay knuckles,
On dull walls strung like wagons,
And tile-red peaks
Despondent in the dry white element.

Night Walkers

Darkness hisses at the town-blocks' end.
Salt-glaze of sleet
Pocks fingers, coldly grits the walks
Sprung flat, like table-knives.

There's a smashed box of wind in every street,
And lamps, for startled hours,
Wistfully guard
Behind their glistening panes shaken with blows
The blanched gold cheeks
Of those we seek for miles sardonically.

Roy Fisher

Script City

Now let me drag the night
Across us like a table,
Over the stove and the fire-irons,

Over the acid light it smothers,
The black shrubs in the forecourt
And our cloudy quiet.

Sleep with me in the ghost
The lamp shed on the dark,
And I'll see that we wake

Late, in a marine city
Strung newly along a bay,
Its white blocks wet with fog;

A place where, quietly,
All scripts are made, and figures,
And words lie down to sleep as we do.

An Unofficial Fisher

Something Unmade

There's something unmade
In the street this morning.

The wind at the door
Comes straight from licking at it,

And the thicket of noise
Contains a new silence.

Something more delicate
Than an egg on the tarmac,

More quiet and bland
Than the milk in the bottle,

prouder than housetops.

If I walk out now
before the street's busy,

Kicking a newspaper
Rolled in a ball

With under one arm
A musical instrument,

It may find things easier.

I would not have it
Left there to grow fractious.

Roy Fisher

Results

Sitting in cafes
For years on end
I have given a certain justice of the eye
To a few things:

To four or five of the glances
Cast my way,
To the loves and indecisions and so forth
Of friends and not-friends.

Now they come around
Like fish in a stream;
Linger a moment for recognition
And leave, unharmed.

Last Brief Maxims

Judge by colours.
Consult the breast,
The groin, the belly;
Make things you can carry.

At each day's end
Laugh at the clock
And die in the squat
Wall of the honeycomb.

Study anatomy.
Sacrifice often
To the weather and women;
Make room for the dead.

Consider how
A second glance
Denies the first
Denies the first.

Roy Fisher

After Midnight

The lamps that clamber
About the moon,
The pinnacles and the parapets.

August carries
A cold in its belly,
After the crowds
Bloated clowns lie in the leaves.

The lamps that clamber
About the moon,
The pinnacles and the parapets.

Traffic lights
Wind down the hours;
An early fog
Filters across the public face.

The lamps that clamber
About the moon,
The pinnacles and the parapets.

An open eye.
Eroded streets.
Trying the doors
A constable finds night unlocked.

The Bachelors Stripped Bare by their Bride

A.B.C. "The three of us discussed your masterpiece—"
D.   "Splendid, my boys! I don't know whether—"
A.B.C. "And we decided we should like to ask—"
D.   "It overheard you; it and I are no longer on
           the best of terms. I have—"
A.B.C. "How far you feel your concept still holds good."
D.   "an idea it disapproves of the use I made of what
           it earned me. That was a happy time!"
A.   "Would you, for instance, do the same again?"
D.   "I couldn't, if I tried. I'm senile. I'm happy too;
           besides, this is a most progressive age and I spend
           all my time with these little . . ."
B.   "Your work was hailed in nineteen-ten as being—"
D.   "They said all sorts of things. I remember
           there were two red-haired brothers—"
C.   "And some of us have still not quite caught up!"
D.   "My dear young friends, remember this: I am a very
           elderly Frenchman. The thing
           that has interested me most through my life
           Is eroticism. God bless us all."
A.B.C. "That doesn't quite—"
D.   "—Including you. Goodnight."

Roy Fisher

Division of Labour

I saw the dustmen drink the light
And remain dry;
I saw the grey wagon of dessication,
While the day raced in rivulets all about it,
Crawling along the gutter like a blind dog.

I thought of an endless night, so deep
That it would slake them,
These parched and red-eyed men,
In flooded shafts and cool sky-valleys:
I wanted them to love that blue mind
For all of us, whose claim on it was less.

Then saw how they were decomposed
Into their dust,
The skin losing its touch and the eyes their distance,
So that they hardly sensed
Even the ripples under the girders of the bridge
They crossed at nightfall going home;

And I remembered how our dreams
Can make themselves only
From what we touch when we are wide awake.

I saw the dustmen drinking light
And the grey wagon of dessication
crawl in the gutter like a blind dog.

An Unofficial Fisher

Uncle Jim's Will

THIS IS the Last Will and Testament of me, Uncle Jim, being in my right mind on the 14th of October 1934. All statements previously made by me regarding my death are hereby cancelled. Any additions, codicils, other wills, etc., I may make in the future are to count for nothing, *whatever they may say*.

I wish my body to be cremated after my death as soon as possible without any religious ceremony or songs or music of any kind, or any person of my acquaintance in attendance. Or near by. Any ashes to be thrown away at once.

I particularly wish my dentures and spectacles (if worn) to be disposed of immediately subsequent to death by way of the ordinary rubbish collection (bin) and not to be tried for size at that time *by anyone at all*.

My clothes, collars, boots, etc., to be sold for a decent price at once *without exception*, the sale to be conducted by a suitable newspaper advertisement without personal particulars.

I BEQUEATH, supposing the articles to be still in my possession at my death, and still of use—

1) All goods not specifically mentioned here below to my wife Doris Mary, if living. If not living, to my mistress, Lois Ivy Thompson. If both not living, the goods to be divided fairly between the remaining beneficiaries below listed, by the clergyman of St. Andrew's Church, Bowman Road, Capon Heath. Or of any other church agreeable to those concerned. If I have, before death, for any reason married a second time, this last procedure to be followed, *notwithstanding*.

2) My hunter watch with chain and my army field glasses in leather case to my brother Will or his heirs.

3) My private collection of photographs, books and magazines kept in the attic of this house, 17 Livingstone Road, in metal toolbox under the dumbbells, to my wife; to be divided equally or as she thinks fit with my eldest son, Horace. Hers to be the first choice in any event.

4) Also to our son Horace the copy of my Birth Certificate mounted and framed in a mount and frame made and embroidered by my mother while lying-in.

5) My certificate (1916) of unfitness for military service to the Imperial War Museum (!).

6) My mistress Lois Thompson to my second son Kenneth without responsibility for maintenance.

7) The stethoscope left at the house by Dr. Dann in 1927 immediately prior to his fatal collapse and accident, to my dear little nephew Roy Fisher, to be kept in trust by his mother.

8) Any moneys whatever remaining in my Savings Deposit Account to my daughter Lilian, provided only that she undertakes to wear her glasses at all necessary times.

9) My swordstick to my youngest son, Stuart, also any protectives remaining from the bulk order made last year, 1933. (Buff packages packed into smaller teachests in attic of 17 Livingstone Road). Also any of same or other personal articles in my pockets at death.

10) My bitch Lucy, to the Capon Heath Canine Home in perpetuity, and to be buried there.

11) My BSA roadster bicycle with box of spare handlebar grips, also the dumbbells in the attic of 17 Livingstone Road, to my sister Edith, for her disposal as she wishes, or the use of her friends.

An Unofficial Fisher

---

12) The picture "Wedded" by Lord Leighton (print) to Mrs. Cooper, Capon Heath Post Office.

13) The set (as new) of croquet mallets in the shed at 17 Livingstone Rd., bequeathed me in the division (1913) of my Uncle Will's property on his death, to my brother Will, or his heirs, for the name's sake.

14) The set of hoops and ball bequeathed me with the above, to my dear little nephew Roy, to go with the stethoscope.

                Witness my hand this 14th day of October 1934

                                  (signed) *Uncle Jim*

Big Girl

Heavy-shouldered,
      slow, like a bull
           advancing into a field,
She walked in a well-cut suit across the concrete,
      nothing in her path at first.

High above her
      enamel-shaded lamps
           swayed under the tin roof;

All around
      the stallholders were clearing up the market
      running in and out of the night
      across, before, behind
           her line of march.

In the middle of all this
      she encountered face to face
           a neat-looking man.

This man she kissed at once: his hands
      appeared around her back, slithering,
while hers hung still against her skirt.

When she jerked her head away he became
      a mark on the floor, or something that disappeared
           among the crates somebody pushed across just then;

Anyway, she walked on
      just as before, till
           reaching the exit

An Unofficial Fisher

She walked up to a small sports car
           and got in. At the wheel was a small leathery old
                    woman who at once reversed out of the side
                    street into the highway without looking and
                    without mishap and drove off fast.

So it didn't really count.

Roy Fisher

The Discovery of Metre

Moving towards
      the multiplication
           of fields
The respectful
      population of his
           surroundings by himself
His tokens
      understood
           his work done
By others without bidding
      his newest thoughts
           read in advance
He took to talking
      at length
           and like
Any old man
      walking downstairs
           three steps
And a pause
      still talking
           pleased to be
Talking and
      still making it
           downstairs.

Abraham Darby's Bridge

Forget the masterpiece itself:
It cracks with watching;
A slow landslide
Shoves at the pier-stones.

And the black spars
Of the ironwork build like joinery,
Cranking the arch out
With a wader-bird's leverage

Meet to support less—only
A tarred, spongy walk
Without even the trade
Of a tourist's fee.

The masterpiece is now
A standing elegy
Masking its old truculence:
Anyway, *that* past is shot.

Yet how we love a bridge—
Bay-breaker or ditchplank,
a dry-eyed span—
Forget the thing itself, though,

Now that it has to be
Torn down for safety
Or turned to a monument;
Reverie all that can conjure

The bustle of the gorge then,
Cargoes on the Severn,

Roy Fisher

Smoke among the bluffs, sooty chimneys
Starting from the wood:

Now an empty railbed
Tracks up the river's course
Past Coalport and Madeley—
Rubbles of the enterprise

With gardens and hovels
Collapsed into peace,
Patched with fresh mortar,
With fresh cinders.

The sky opens to the north,
Rods bow under the elders;
On the valley, the scorch-marks
Look small and honourable.

But spit into the wind,
The century after next returns it:
To the played-out heap
Colonies are coming.

An Unofficial Fisher

'Dear Gael'

'Dear Gael,

           I hear you've called Roy Fisher
"the most *distinguished* living Midlands poet".
I may be a wee bit dim
away from it all up here, but I mean
distinguished from *what*?
—distinguished from anything worth bothering about
I should have thought.

It's too much, when you've wheedled the price of a Sunday paper
out of someone you thought was a friend
to find that poetical *grocer*
smirking in a photo with his fellow toadies—
this man who makes out he's a *hermit*
looking like nothing so much
as a miscegenation by George MacBeth
out of Hugh MacDiarmid—

Perhaps you could just *explain* to me in a word or two
or let me in on the wheeze
of why you've turned to providing free copy
for Lucie-Smith and the other *Lucies*?
When they've sucked your blood and mine
can't you just hear them chortle?
You ought to take heed of another Sassenach—
the one called Aristotle:

for I'm planning a wee katharsis—
like, *you give* me *the pity*
and I'll give you *the fright,*
and don't suppose that if you do nothing but stay on your arses
you'll still be all right . . .'

Roy Fisher

'Neighbours, We'll Not Part Tonight!'

The Demon Knitters of Dent

Roll me round to the stories of the great knittings
that took place in the foretimes
in a smell of straw and peat in smoky kitchens

with a 'clack' for a sound
we're knitting the houses round

As the sun's great sheep's eye slunk down behind the fell
and his thick grey blanket folded its long rows over
door after door closed soft as the mighty strode,
staggered, ran, limped in the dark to their knitting spell

with a step for a sound
we're knitting the houses round

There was Ramsback Rachel, Black Tick and Tam Tup,
Six-Pin Tirleyman (twisty Gannelbon's grandson)
Little Stitch Baby and Kitty Curl, Granny Pullock with the straddle legs
and a long pale idiot man who would knit with his toes: these made the
    party up

with a breath for a sound
we're knitting the houses round

Then came the girls Pocket and Flitty, and Ribber Wagstaff with his
    strong thumbs,
Giantess Appleyard in ten petticoats and not perspiring
and Schoolmaster Weazell with his knitted walking-stick
come to set all the children their knitting sums

An Unofficial Fisher

with a squeeze for a sound
we're knitting the houses round

Where was the clicking of laughter than but amid the smoke
when the knitting songs and the knitting stories ran free
and the mutton-grease fumbled the wool
and the wool-swaddled babes in the cockloft started to choke?

With a cough for a sound
we're knitting the houses round

When it's long past midnight and the yards of knitting enfold
foot upon stamping foot, not gingerly pressed together
and the flushed pink faces still mouth out the rows of song
then the joy of the knitting runs stitches through young and old

with a gasp for a sound
we're knitting the houses round

Then the needles fly faster and faster: wondrous rows fall
like foam on the beck from those long-labouring fingers;
pile on the floor to the last knitting hymn round knees, waists, bosoms
       and clasp
all the great passionate ones in one soft breathing pall

with a sociable silence
we're knitting the houses round

Art Comes to its Senses Again

'The generosity of an anonymous corporate donor makes it possible for this year's prize to be trebled in value and to include share options. Accordingly the award will be genre-specific and will need to bear directly on the title provided by the panel.

The award will be made to a work entitled:

Old Man Swallowing His Tongue

On this occasion the work will be in **one** of the following genres:

    a sculptural group, four-fifths life-size

    a folk opera in two acts, for soloists, chamber orchestra and optional chorus

    a painted ceiling

    a string quartet

    a non-figurative but quite colourful painting

    a heroic piano piece of between fifteen and nineteen minutes' duration

Specifically excluded from consideration will be works submitted in any of the following forms: solo dance-pieces, video installations, interactive DVDs, netsuke, preserved human tissue, poems.'

An Unofficial Fisher

A Poetry List

The Appian Way in full swing. Lined with the marble tombs of the illustrious dead and rows of crucified gladiators.

a poet's poets' anthology

FLEUR ADCOCK

An 80th Birthday Card for Roy

Happy birthday! I'm sorry this is not
that clutch of long-tailed tits you always wanted
or a melodious charm of goldfinches.
They would certainly fly more gracefully
than my stumbling public-private poem
(you know how tricky such commissions are—
although you'd bring to them your customary
elegance, intelligence and wit).

In any case, you're doing all right for birds:
swallows dashing out from under your eaves,
thrushes and a blackbird both nesting
outside your kitchen window.
                                  Here, I see,
I should slip in a flattering metaphor
about your lyric voice. It wouldn't be apt:
your poems are not songs; they are to think with.
Thank you for them; and not for them only.

I could start reminiscing—Arvon courses,
Bucharest, Burton Dassett, the Marsden hat—
but you know all that; and it's your birthday.
Happiness, we've agreed, tends more and more
these days to be bird-shaped. For a present,
if I can manage teletransportation,
I'll zoom a pair of kingfishers your way;
or a golden oriole; a Phoenix.

ANN ATKINSON

Driving Home from Grasmere

'There are in our existence spots of time
Which with distinct pre-eminence retain
A renovating Virtue, whence our minds
Are nourished and invisibly repaired.'
                The Prelude XI

You'd kept a thread of story spinning
down the M6 and through Cheshire,
over Macclesfield, past the Cat and Fiddle,
then we'd cut onto the track across Axe Edge.
You pointed—there the Dane gathers its water,
here, spoil heaps where Buxton men scraped coal—
poor stuff, enough to boil a kettle, warm a hearth.

It might have been at Thirkelow Rocks
or maybe the cairn on High Edge, but
we rounded the bend and stark on the crest
three horses were massive against the sky.
Something burned deep in the mind,
both of us, silent and clasping hands.

Did we slow then to see them lessen
down a shifting perspective, or tame them
with a story—the woman who said, *see those trees,
when there's rain on the way they come near—*
but I let go your hand and we carried on home.
A clear sky, the moon, at its perigee that night,
rolled full and close on our horizons.

ELEANOR COOKE

Nettle Soup

There are precedents for these undertakings—
turn straw into gold,
weave a shirt from thistles with your bare hands,
wash away the blood in a dry well.

I can do none of these.
I bring you nettle soup.

I should have picked the nettles in the spring.
That's the best time for nettles,
when they're young and sweet. The children
went down the field—

I'm talking years ago—
to gather nettles,

tucked their trousers into their boots, put on gloves.
When the soup was made
they were chary at first, lifting spoon to lip,
letting it in, drop by drop.

They laughed to find
it didn't sting their tongues.

Now the year turns and it's late for nettles,
but I found these beside the stream—
a second flush where I'd picked—March,
was it, April?

So after all, it's not too late
to make nettle soup,

Eleanor Cooke

though there won't be enough here to bag up
for the freezer. You took some out,
de-frosted it for lunch—remember?—
and it was good.

But this I bring you's fresh,
the late leaves pale at the tip

when I picked them. I didn't notice the stings
at the time, but look:
the rash they raised along my skin's
still raw.

I'll leave the soup here on the table.
Don't let it go cold.

KELVIN CORCORAN

The Fisher Piano

Elytis
Evans, George
Evans, Paul
Ferlinghetti
Peter Finch
Half a pound
Of tupenny rice
Alec Finlay
Roy Fisher

I know exactly where you are
above my head and two feet to the right
gutting a sequence magnanimous.

    *

On national day in our new/old nation young men
parade and hoist aloft dusted off banners,
muscular white gloves gripping splintered poles.

(last year we cancelled, we had no tweezers, no glue)

Black haired country girls launch red roses,
up up and the sepia image, slightly distorted, flutters:
Poetry Champion Sits At His Piano—Our Hero.

    *

Roy—is that you out there, above the tin-ear merchants,
flash buggers and lickspittles in their dark workshops,
in a decent country called the possibilities of poetry?

Kelvin Corcoran

Chords go clattering along Kentish Road heading out,
ride your bike with your dad, untranslate the Soho works
the syntax of canals and the naming of the poor.

Zig-zagging exponent of the ordinary idiom of wonder,
as true as the awkward fact with half of England
in a ring of cities arranged without fuss or pomp.

The headline starts from the Guardian sprite—
Sullivan Bids Bittersweet Farewell To Birmingham
Fisher Drives His Piano Down The Handsworth Loop.

(left hand steady on the towpath)

PETER DIDSBURY

A Closing Prospect

Sudden exhilaration
of late morning sun in the backstreets.
The late winter or early spring as it may be
morning sunlight. My car
corners in the keen air, seemingly with intent,
leaps forward to land on the iron bridge
which spans the muddy drain.
A chain-link fence glints dully on the left,
a hundred yards or so of it holding back
a ragged and half-hearted crowd of thorns,
muffled with torn festoons of carrier bag.
I suddenly see myself
returning by night to stand beneath cold stars,
with kerosene, to walk a cleansing line of flame
along the reflective running parallel waters.
I might simply be imagining
what the summer, given time, will accomplish anyway,
but it doesn't feel like that. It feels like joy,
a joy that has sat down next to me
in the empty passenger seat.
I think I could become quite passionate about hedgerows.
The thought seems to function
as an acceptance of things as they are,
which is incomprehensible
(and perhaps irrevocable).
When the last corner affords a closing prospect
of my office windows, high in a corner of the old school,
Victorian alms-houses' court and clock tower next to it,
I even flirt with the idea
that I could come to be reconciled
to having to go through the whole damn thing again,

Peter Didsbury

---

the whole long shameful business and waste of breath,
if only for the sake of turning slowly
through these gates one more time,
between their brick piers, to park, then sit a while,
then step from my rapidly cooling vehicle
out into such a morning, such an amazement of light.

LAURIE DUGGAN

The London Road

1

rough joins where beams from ships
slot into the neighbour walls;

intrusions of ironmongery
behind the curtains

the sun at an angle
manages the northern window

half-illumined furniture trapped
by slight twists, each wall a false perspective

striations in an enormous fireplace

a dark house intersected by light

2

a
cloud
moves
over
a
yellow
field

drips hang on the underbase of a bird bath

3

at the edge of town a car yard and an archaeological excavation
toward Londinium, on Watling Street
over the hill, Stone Chapel, the dry valley of Syndale

stinging nettle, dead nettle, dock, cow parsley, goose grass
    (near North Street)

forget-me-not, buttercup, stitchwort
    (near Plumford)

at the edge of town
remains of the hospice
that once bridged the Roman road:
Ospringe

(and there is a spring,
a channel under the floor
of the Maison Dieu

westward,
hands pull rope around a sheaf of
what?
wheat? asparagus?
Lamb's Conduit
FOUNDED 1843

old hinges of a former door
painted over

a poet's poets' anthology

PETER HUGHES

Poly-Olbion

& this pub goes back to the last ice age
when Brutus ambled into Buckfastleigh
clanked sacks of silverware onto the bar
& ordered brioches & cappuccini

my great-grandfather was Aeneas
he boomed   to the bright strains of a French march
soon Spanish brandy seethed between us
Al Pacino glowing around the bay

so many separate blue receptors
debating permissible harmonics
& whether English is fit for singing
but at Christmas it remains the custom

to soak a goose's neck in lard & whisky
before sliding it into a mason

SIÂN HUGHES

City

I knew the city would never make sense to me
so the long queue of buses outside the cathedral
and the hotel of brown carpeting and salesmen,
the lift in an old green Cortina from the forecourt
to a block of flats where I sign a six months contract
on a room with a tall window and share of a bathroom
where hot water is dished out in 20p portions
from a dodgy meter on the landing were all fine with me
considering, all I expected was constriction
and statues of it built behind the band stand in Rotten Park.

What surprised me was the long view from the fifteenth floor
where the landlord sat me under a row of gold awards
framed on the remains of a knocked-through partition wall,
won in his days in the City Centre Post Office, for valour
in the face of a series of armed hold-ups over giros
and unpaid pensions; the way the city never met in the middle
but grouped itself hopefully from one clump of green to another
as far as the prison and the Fire Salvage shop, further even
than the circle line that would take me home a different way
over and over again. And what comes back, even now

the old police station place where I signed on has long gone,
and the cafes where I ordered milky coffee and fifty pence of curry
in a plastic bowl have closed, even the old ladies who dealt in
sausage sandwiches behind the porn cinemas, it's metamorphosis,
the part where she sleeps in the day, in the stillness, and the long
     afternoon
where I was barely a mark on the silence, turning my face to a rented wall
while the old man taps on my door for his visitors, his messages,
and none of us go to his funeral, not even Maggie, who was the one

climbed a broken ladder from the outhouse to let him in his room
          that time
he lost his key. She was six months pregnant, never missed a step.

AUGUST KLEINZAHLER

Attach To A Place

Attach to a place
It attaches to you
And the land around
Comes through
The windows, stonework
Weather blowing in
Rattling the glass
Your own pushing back
Ah, and there's the making
Of some turbulence
Over there
Where
In your left shoe
A wee cyclone
And there, too
To the right of the cabinet
Where the cat
Might choose, midday, to nap
The cat
The cat
Outside in the rain
Has he a place to hide
Oh, yes
Oh, my, yes

R. F. LANGLEY

Aftermath

When you wake up it has been raining.
The angel holds up one forefinger,
levels the other at your chest.

Guess.

From the cold Adam, now,
and from the infant silent in the air,

                    the droplets
                    resting on the threads,

                    the residue of breath
                    left in your ear.

Guess from the spark
in the foliage.

                    How did a shower sound to him,
                    in the Jewellery Quarter?

                    With his pronouns?

                    They did a brisk trade
                    in chrysoprase?

And this one, which you did not hear
last night, making itself with weather
that you slept through?

The angel saw it pass over.
Raised a finger.

R.F. Langley

Counting into the quiet.

Counting into the quiet.
Looking you in the eye.

ANGELA LEIGHTON

Sheep Count

A wrong turn somewhere, mismatch, off the map's
hyphened footpaths, contours, its quaint names—

Dollywaggon Pike, Seat Sandal, Fairfield—here,
a nameless grassy plain in mist and rain,

a world expressly itself, unmarked by signs,
unless, on the ground, where something's come apart,

you read those whitened bones widespread like gifts:
tibula, scapula, vertebra, humerus, ribs,

and the skull, lightweight, its serious burden shed,
nuzzling the grass that sews it back to earth.

Such odds and ends, the fellow creature known
in outline only, punctuated form,

as if it made another kind of map,
for going nowhere, losing, giving up,

as if those furtive waymarks showed how far
from anywhere, neither here nor there, we are,

lost from the start perhaps, in weather and cold,
and the shepherd gone who called the count or score:

yan tyan tethera methera pimp
sethera lethera hovera dovera dick.

JOHN MATTHIAS

Longs and Shorts

And will a photograph save us? We're old enough
To have had a temptation to think
That the old cliché about *ars longa* had some
Actual merit. What's long
Are the drifting sands as we plod to the
Music of *vita brevis*. But it *is* a music, tra-la.
It seems but a moment ago you were only 70
And we urged you in your words to
Put the piano at risk, to left-hand us a poem.
But photography's the democratic art.
I just saw a snap of you in South Bend, Indiana
The very night of your reading in 1980.
It was also the first night you'd spent outside
Of Britain: Not in Paris, not in Rome, but
South Bend, Indiana. I can't even say it's the
Midwestern Manchester, although you
Liked and found familiar the "abandoned workings,"
As W.H. Auden would say, of the old
Studebaker auto plant. After the reading we
Travelled out to the house of a prof
In the same car with another guest of the school
Who seemed even more laid-back
Than you, though also a bit incongruous.
He too both wrote and put the piano at risk. He too
Had a cosmopolitan soul. At the party
You sat together on a sofa—clearly someone
Would play. As you jazzed the *vita brevis*
Out of the upright, *Ars Longa* himself
Appeared with his camera. And here in
A short book is the picture long after the music
Has fled. I can see it's my friend Roy Fisher

Fishing for the right notes in a riff.
But the caption grasping at by god immortal life
Declaims like Caesar's newsboy: *John Cage
Plays four minutes of silence*
While on the opposite page Harold Brodkey's
Mislabeled *Joseph Brodsky*.
Irreversible, Roy. But what the hell?

IAN McMILLAN

The Literary Life

An upper room of a pub in 1980:
Roy Fisher is sitting in a corner
Getting ready to read poems.

I have just read some poems
And later I will remember this
As one of my first poetry readings;

During it a man tried to sell vegetables
And another man, drunk, shouted
I'll kill that bastard if he doesn't stop selling vegetables

And someone else shouted *the drink*
The drink has destroyed him! And the novelist
Jack Trevor Story ran into the room

Shouting *People I am The President*
And he was wearing a flying helmet and a cape.
Roy looked at me across the room and said
This is The Literary Life: get used to it.

PETER MIDDLETON

The Walls

Pompeii walls bricked in a civilized life
where stone now shows through bird and water frescoes

how could television be more quick than the room
you'll want to give these beautiful vanishing images forever

what have you got on and what's on do you know
those big embarrassing bodies brother to those grand designs

our guest on the box shows a delightful extended family dinner
furnishes time with an ironic slipcover

narrative brushes goods we really must buy
and learn to say thank you thank you seduce me again

then we can talk to each other about what we saw
the drama will make like conversation

isn't glass full of wonder you can hardly see the grey
outside the picture actors leave history for their own four walls

MICHAEL O'NEILL

Never

Never drive through the rain
                                  slogging back as last weekend
from a Liverpool
                 that widens to a glimpse
of the river's grey
                 indomitable sheen
or narrows down
                 to the terminus of age
no one any younger
                 never drive through the rain
wipers fretting but
                 'It won't do. It beckons'
plays a downcast music
                 a steadfast music
as it did in perhaps no
                 definitely our first issue.

Never use '*I* or *you*'
                 rarely absent from my efforts
than your ghosts prod me
                 those courteous virtual ghosts
sitting with their milk
                 before the thunder peals
waiting even now for the
                 gang of selves and non-selves
I'd call these lines to walk
                 across the poem's stage-set
vanish into the wings
                 then relax and maybe share a joke.

TOM PICKARD

the short eared owl as ground nesting metaphor

Roy Fisher said
owl is low
spelt inside out.

L flaps to the front
and the W,
hatched
and flown back,
splays
like a tail
over O
rolled
and nestled

waiting
to
toowoo
again.

RALPH PITE

from walesandbordertrains

      1

  over magnolia and mauve
tree-shadows
   gliding as we move.

mistletoe spheres
   like snared balloons
planetary
   lantern shells

   their outlines
pale as myriad
   river as
riverbank clays.

ploughed field's
   stainless water-panes
cloud stepping-stones.

[…]

TRANSONANCE

in wheels' whirl
through bedded rail
walkaround
and engine noise

outriding wave
through shoots and

branches strands
of the entire

even across fractional
gaps that cushion joins.

catspaw ripples
a reptile skin
among measures of swell
goods train bulk
materials sleeper
Pendolino

these larger surges dampened
and absorbed in inland
foliating estuaries of disused
shunting-yards

quiver into
colonizing trees.

[…]

STRETTON

a sinewy orchard.

passengers alight
finally
to car-park hurry
back as

breathless
checked worry
wills forth obstacles:

Ralph Pite

smoke's translucence,
oily and dark
field boundary streams

through hazel low
and penetrating

winter light.

IAN POPLE

A View of Arnhem

The light is patterned
and shaping round the fields,
or coming from the corner,
an unmade sun among boxes.
On the garden side,
you might shutter off
the windows, for the lake
is uncomfortable,
the water high, pouring
and contained, there
among the formal trees,
the stiff grass flattened
and open towards
the cars and courtyard.

The hillsides move
through one another
and little figures
through the light and trees,
the river in the moonlight.
The sheep are walking
by the water wheel;
behind the chain link
fencing, laurel,
rhododendron, a tree
that's bitten to the quick
by lightning, where the dog
looks up at the man
and the man looks
down at the dog.

Ian Pople

And there'll be one
winnowing and another
binding sheaves,
and another sitting
at lunch because
they'll know,
cramped as they are,
if someone turns
or someone smiles.

RICHARD PRICE

Jazz Syllabus

The electric piano
just then. The left, the right

apart from everything else.
Harpsichord or Church?

The left and the right,
Harpsichord
or Grand Piano 2.

Strawberry-scented strawberry coloured
raspberry nail varnish,

a smear on one off-white key.
'Bursting in on me like that.'

TOM RAWORTH

Got On

fuck the friendly image
seen from destruction
and decay

eating electricity

pockets of warmth

life constructed
to tap thought
newton
affected by gravity
work to decay

graphic audio
a movie in your mind
famous historian by committee

standard sets

rivets of instance
exception as possibility
pop hen

smaller in the world

protect peace

to have so little
cur parade
common flame

a poet's poets' anthology

---

stretch focus
moon mirror reflection

through glass
wonders to perform
photography

give objects memory

no history
gutter
alone at dinner

filters disappear

hope shapes that thaw

PETER RILEY

Bay of Argus

The narrow shore, barely room to walk
between sea and the tall fences
of the orange groves. Warm wind,
cloudy day on the stones *and suffering
shall cease* and we all return to some
pre-Aurignacian repletion, something to
do / something for now / something to
end all this, advance / torment.

Squeezed between land and sea the path ends.
A dark town across the bay, clumps
of giant fennel (carrier of fire) and we turn back
one by one we turn home, knowing
we hold a rightness in the bones of the hand
waiting for a musical instrument to articulate it.
We call for a task, a fidelity, a fire to carry home
and who hears us?

Roy Fisher hears me, up in the northern hills,
and turns to pat the dog that died.

This poem is a re-inscription of the prose poem in Greek Passages *(Shearsman Books, 2009), p.44.*

PETER ROBINSON

Unearned Visuals

That bungalow protected by Decaux hoardings,
a one-off industrial cottage has
two chimney pots, bayed windows,
the green door in between them
and lemon-daubed brickwork, smutted now;
it blanks me, close up, appears to hide
behind those images.

Its grey net curtains and metal-stud door,
steep roof-slope, lemon brick, what's behind?
I've never seen anyone enter or leave,
just looking, on the way to work.
In gravel pit lodge, as was,
not a thing's astir.

Past crescent shops where trams would turn,
stood forward of the building line
it's hidden from package holiday vistas,
spectacular bank accounts, high definition
pay-as-you-watch-them franchise wars …
weekend supplement pages!

That cottage concealed behind Decaux hoardings
has a yard screened by their dark side.
After working, I think you'll find,
here in the shadow of a bigged-up world,
unearned, though it seems to hide
like rain-smell coming from an overcoat,
the actual imagined.

ROBERT SHEPPARD

Tentatives

Between buildings brushed
By bitter wind

Bodies chatter
Chilled equivocation

Sliced by splintered screen
Of sinking reflections

As some else
Thing resonates

A minor chord
Among flurries tinkling

Lost in
Tingles of thing

Hoist from the purest
Lyric a catch

To pull up the stepped lines
Silvered in living daylights

A neck ridged with bone barely
Turning on a pillow breathing fast

Obstinate anchorage
Slowly

Turning

Wind cuts sunlight
Leaf-glitter tells you it's there

Pushes so hard it could bend
Light if you chose to believe

      which you do it makes it
      cowl like a bush in a gust curling

Its own grey withdrawal
Terrified of its black heart
Sun's low disk
Sinks

Throws long shadows lawns of
Dark stretching back from flaming

Brickwork the faces of buildings
Distant towers

Glint buckled fire for a
Second then gutter

Lost reclaimed
By the order of place some

Where at the periphery stretches
A god created by gospels

That thread between things
Like gossamer like culture

January–May 2008

JEFFREY WAINWRIGHT

The Painter

The painter is our see-er and starts always from infinity.
She looks at the plane and everything is there.
That is why it must be filled with what
We others know, with our familiars.

Quick! A woman in a chair leaning rightwards
With the other arm akimbo. Quick! A cow
Recumbent in a field, a distant copse, a fence.
Quick! A boathouse, a jetty, a shingle beach.
Quick! Flowers! Quick! Thistles! Quick! Sumptuous flowers!

These are what she shows us but less than what she sees,
And how much she wants us to see this.
Then the woman rises from her chair and ambles away—
She is real but she is gone. The cow levers itself upwards
And ambles away, off-stage, gone. We go.

But the painter is undismayed,
For the endless curvatures remain,
And the rational angles, and the colours
Which are what they are but never hold steady
In the light, or, always holding their shapes,
Slip like screens, one behind another,
Signalling from the depths, another green refracting green.

'I am not painting my mind,' she says,
'I am painting what is. Please be with me.
It is good.'

JOHN WELCH

Builders

Is it someone wearing a badge,
Is sad behind a logo, a sort of failed dignity?
It's on his back where he can't reach to scratch,
A man who slows, where summer wastes
An enormous strength down here—
The building workers, ranged along a wall
Are bodies, being as if
Each sculpted out of idleness
And into a frieze of moments
Tattooed, like something
That waits to be deciphered
And a single earring's cheeky gold.
The dust each man
Is carrying in his skin
In every fold and crevice
Will be washed off as if it were the money
That flows away from him
But now for a moment something
Archaic comes to mind
Here in the noon silence,
Its sense of a commanding presence.

DAVID WHEATLEY

Drypool in Old Photographs

1

The man on the corner repeats
at intervals down the street,
as though in a trick photographer's

loop: hands on hips, in fob
pockets, ignoring the see-through dog
ghosting along the pub wall

behind him feeding on air,
on the ghost of a promise
of gristle and bone.

2

Dawn in the brewery yard
finds ice on the dung,
the dray-horse's breath

steaming into the lens.
The barrels tumble chiming
into riverside cellars

and are sprung in a week;
the drayman's further-off
judgment day promises

the bump and jolt of a cemetery
clearance and only then
the vile dust settled at last.

3

The dog and I fall into step.
Peer through his vitreous ribs
and watch the brickwork rewind,

decade on decade. Does he
want feeding? There aren't
shadows enough to sate him.

Sharp against my ribs too,
the ghost of a torn-down future
pushes, prods, and will out.

JOHN WILKINSON

Trades & Crafts

Jingle harness knew the way to go,
a nostrum, a needful.

In cotton mills near Halifax
a bobbin-doffer spins between spindles,

her feet slap the iron floor,
she signals to Jen through the racket.

Joint compound. Greenboard
with its foil surface. Din diminishes, seep

will be controlled, the transport appears,
gabby shadows pitch in,

deputed to their work benches,
billeted behind stucco walls, calling.

Rubble infill was deposited
within exact lines, palladian true,
not time-lines or archaeological layers,
but imputed calls, a curlew

shored up by such studding,
buoyed up by such shadows,

lead-blue that stains the falsework
& sustains also. Rubble had been
whistled through & knocked
with felted hammers. Half attuned to.

Butcher, baker, fishmonger
danced among osiers, their straggled line,

basket weavers waded in the thick.
Your call of course. Your call.

the fisher syndrome explained

ROY FISHER
Death by Adjectives

Being a response in the form of a review to the gift of the millennial reissue of Columbia's Piano Moods *albums*

Piano Moods is a dated title, dragged forward fifty years, and there's plenty of genuine historical interest to be found in George Avakian's account of the early evolution of the microgroove compilation and in the work of the twelve pianists then enlisted, with others, to service its needs. The pianist Dick Katz's essay gives an expert, sometimes tolerant, view of what goes on. The original idea was to set up montages of continuous piano playing and there's a good deal of obliging amenity-music here, by pianists no longer much heard. But some of the work, and the most valuable, doesn't fit the uniform, which gets ripped apart. The sets by Hines, Sullivan and Wilson are important jazz records and always have been: the Tatum concert is still a towering masterpiece.

Earl Hines's ways of opening the music out and knocking it right along always seem to me more consistently audacious than his once-celebrated gambles with time and phrasing. When the tracks by Hines were first issued as 78s and on LP they were said to show the great innovator of the twenties in the placidity of middle age. Huh. There's little rest for the listener here, and no somnambulism by the pianist. He lets Al McKibbon's bass and the wonderful stealthy drumming of J. C. Heard, the sound of 42nd Street in the forties, vamp for him while he goes wherever he wants. There's nothing in jazz like the romping up-tempo passages in *You Can Depend on Me* and *I Hadn't Anyone Till You*, where he lopes relentlessly away with the left while grabbing jagged, sidelong treble phrases apparently out of nowhere. In fact they're out of the pretty plain harmonic progressions, but by no route anybody could have foreseen. This is why intelligent musicians took to playing jazz.

Teddy Wilson, by catching the spirit of what the horn players were moving into, wrote almost the whole working vocabulary of swing piano, opening it up to virtually everybody in the business and seeing it carried on right through bop by Hank Jones and Tommy Flanagan, and all the pianists who favoured open lines: a whole long generation. At his peak between the mid-thirties and mid-forties, he's caught here still in splendid form, before the setting in of the gradual, gentle, apparently painless decline which saw his music lose its edge of timing and structure: its jazz, in short.

Jess Stacy's regarded with considerable affection by followers of the swing bands and small Dixieland groups he played with, and this is somewhat surprising, since his austere, purposeful playing, with its steely touch and introspective bass lines, can be quite forbidding. Rarely an ingratiating melodist, he goes for direct drive, with an unparalleled sense of lift. He was at his best when responding to a band, climbing his way up from under and dominating the proceedings without using cheap tricks. Left to himself without that challenge, he was sometimes liable to wander rather than develop, and the solos here, taken from a number of sessions with a very crisp Hollywood rhythm section, make good listening without often reaching classic status. One memorable oddity is what must be the briskest version of Beiderbecke's *In a Mist* ever recorded.

Ralph Sutton, though not always audibly kind to pianos, is kind to tunes, often venerable and neglected ones: a gentleman escort who could give these old ladies a good time to the point of breathlessness but without lasting physical damage. His numbers tend to be springy workouts, with only rare improvisatory surprises. I've heard a more inventive and intricate American pianist refer to him ironically as 'Ralph Subtle', and he was never an imaginative or emotional heavyweight, but you certainly hear a piano getting thoroughly played, and with two large hands. And for all the gung-ho, he's no thug: these are harmonically sound and balanced keyboard arrangements.

The selection of Fats Waller's fragmentary, back-of-envelope sketches posthumously worked up to performing level, with some lacunae filled, by his friend Joe Sullivan provide no opportunity for the magnificent brooding that often characterised Sullivan's playing. Even Fats's most successful tunes tend to be catchy bat-and-ball sets of two-bar (or, as in *Ain't Misbehavin'* and *Honeysuckle Rose*, one-bar) phrases, and some of these scraps, like *What's Your Name?*, are made from only the most basic of musical materials. But *There'll Come a Time When You'll Need Me* is a serviceable standard, and *Breezin'* is a pretty finger-routine tune Willie the Lion Smith could have written. Maybe he did, one night. Other piano players like to play this one. Sullivan makes no gesture towards Fats's engaging pneumatic bounce, but does

the fisher syndrome explained

all of it his own declamatory way, with a ringing, conclusive account of each number, accompanied by bass and the happy drumming of the like-minded George Wettling. The vigour displayed is sometimes astonishing, particularly in the up-tempo ride-outs, where he smashes on through with (fortunately) an air of complete conviction. If Hines at one time played Armstrong on the piano, Sullivan, as well as being the John Ford of the piano, is Wild Bill Davison and all his Commodores.

I've always been interested in tracking down the under-recorded musicians who stayed around Chicago after the Goodman-Krupa-Freeman-Stacy-Spanier-Wettling-Tough wave had moved out to the swing bands and Eddie Condon's New York circle: one of them was Max Miller, sometimes praised but elusive on record. Hearing him at last I was disappointed. His set runs to rather heavy, tricksy pianistics: these aren't nice ideas. From occasional passages I get a sense that under the show, or ten years back from it, there are the remains of a useful Chicago-Dixieland player like Floyd Bean or Tut Soper, but that wasn't what he was about in this context.

Miller was primarily a commercial studio pianist, as were Buddy Weed, Stan Freeman and Bill Clifton. The occupational hazard of studio musicians is that although they stay clear of dud venues, get paid and keep in wonderful technical shape, they spend their lives actually listening to the garbage they play, and it gets into the bloodstream. Weed plays deftly and agreeably, but it's background music foregrounded, and the patterns on the wallpaper get obtrusive. Clifton, though, is a find, a splendid executant who deals out good standard tunes with an obvious care for piano sound and a contained sense of taste. He reaches for the idiom of the time—easy bebop, Shearing—and doesn't do anything very original, but had he spent longer in the public eye with the Goodman and Herman bands he would certainly have attracted a following. The bandleader Eddie Heywood can be studied with this group. An accomplished pianist of great fluency, he has an incisive touch (beautifully recorded here, as are most of the sets) to rival Tatum's or Nat Cole's, making you think he's about to play jazz—only he never does.

Stan Freeman plays jazz quite often during his eight numbers, but does some terrible things in between. This set's instructive in the light it throws back on the temptations facing keyboard players in the days before synthesizers took over the temptation business and ran with it. In fact, the old hazards bear a great similarity to what's now behind the coloured preset programme buttons on a big home synthesizer—Latin, Classical, Country and Western, Hip Hop, Bossa Nova, Kletzmer, Jazz. 'Jazz' is an effect you can turn on for half a chorus and drop. This is what Freeman, in what sounds like a wholly scored trio showcase set, does. He has fantastic technique and a masterful musical intelligence, and much of the music is well worth attention. But not for long at a stretch. He goes off into waltzes, bits of Boccherini and stretches of Old Music Master twaddle, glitteringly played. The whole thing sounds like a piano company product-demonstration sampler.

In the early fifties Erroll Garner, Ahmad Jamal and Joe Bushkin (already a youthful veteran of the bands of Berigan, Goodman and Tommy Dorsey) were doing the prudent thing and making themselves popular. In an outwardly smooth era, brand-identity and packaging held the keys, with residencies, concert tours and Songbook albums taking the place of ballroom one-nighters, juke-box singles and jam sessions. It was a time of high-class novelties—the Gerry Mulligan Quartet, the Dave Brubeck Quartet, J and K, the MJQ, the Chico Hamilton Quintet—mostly in the tradition of Artie Shaw's restless innovations of a generation earlier. The solo pianists didn't lean so much towards classical ideas, but they tended to stress their marketable idiosyncrasies. Garner's set is bright and entertaining. Every number is, as always, Garnerised, but the soul of the Mighty Wurlitzer he carried incongruously within his slight frame is kept in bounds here. Jamal's trademark was eloquent minimalism, at which he was very good indeed. It depended on immaculate trio playing and pinpoint swing, and this set's exemplary. Bushkin, the least eccentric of these, was always a quite decorative, sometimes narcissistic player (if Hines was the Armstrong of the piano and Sullivan was the Wild Bill Davison, Bushkin was the Ruby Braff) but nevertheless perpetually carried a very respectable jazz kick, even when pleasing the diners.

Tatum's Shrine concert is well known. There's nothing left to say about Tatum, except perhaps that (a) the more you listen to him the less cloying he gets, because (b) he just swung more than anybody else.

GEORGINA HAMMICK

Roy Fisher, letter-writer

The first time Roy and I met we were reading our poems in a tent. I don't recall what the reading was in aid of, or why we were under canvas—what stays with me is the cold. An arctic wind blew through the flaps and all of us, readers and audience, froze. 'It was Siberian,' Patricia Beer wrote to me afterwards. 'If I hadn't had my fur coat, I should have had pleurisy; I should have made a point of it . . .' Better than Patricia's fur coat that day I remember Roy's jacket, dark blue with a furry orange lining, and my asking him what he was doing wearing my son Tom's anorak I'd bought the week before at the Army & Navy Stores.

That was thirty-four years ago, and now we're asked to believe that Roy's about to be eighty, which I wouldn't were I not following closely behind. To mark his birthday, and celebrate his poetry and prose, I'd hoped to break my duck and write him a poem. But poems, never much cop in any case, abandoned me long ago, and none chose to oblige. What did arrive, and repeated itself, was two lines: *Dear Roy/ Attaboy*—hardly the stuff for a *festschrift*, and a deal too mushy for R F, though I knew the things they embraced, and what I meant by them.

Unable to come up with a poem, and with deadlines approaching, I turned to the letters Roy wrote to me, sporadically, over the years. (He writes e-mails now, which I don't do, so these days when we communicate it's by telephone.) Anyone who's corresponded with Roy in the days of old-style pen-and-ink will know the unchanging character of his envelope: a white GL, the kind that takes a three-times-folded sheet of A4, some with University of Keele in the top left-hand corner, all with the recipient's name and address, in his unmistakable hand, centrally and precisely placed. Roy's calligraphy, forward leaning, graceful, controlled—but with every now and then a looping and wayward flourish—derives, I imagine, from his adolescence, and the painter/graphic artist he was then hoping to be. I asked him once how a left-hander was able to manage such stylish precision on the page (the left margins so sharp you'd think them ruled; the undeviatingly exact line spaces), but his patient and factual answer was no help at all.

'I'm sorry you have discomforts too,' Roy wrote to me in 1978, apropos of some anxiety I no longer recall. 'The children of Gemini need to turn to one another to be believed in such moods. I think there are those who consider us able to wriggle sideways out of any trouble, and into some other selves of ourselves that we have.' Roy's letters, written in a range of Geminian moods, and who knows what selves, cover a range of subject matter, though rereading them all at one sitting I can spot recurring themes. Work in progress, or work not progressing; his garden, and what's growing, or refusing to grow, in it, the specifics of his vegetable patch often accompanied by a quirky horticultural aside: 'Did you know camellias were deciduous if the wind's strong enough?' His wider landscape, its geology, seasons and weather, features too, in singular, atmospheric and painterly ways. What follows is the opening paragraph of a letter that reached me in March 1984 from Eleven Steps, Upper Hulme:

'The news is that this morning the little valleys and wrinkles of this barren upland are populated by those travelling finger-like mists that have a Japanese name which I've forgotten: they're supernatural entities that come to gather the souls of the dead. I don't know who they're after. Old Mr Tunnicliffe, my near neighbour (three-quarters of a mile) died at last of his farmer's lung a few weeks ago, but if they're after him, they're pointing the wrong way. They are, in fact, most personal-looking beings. Some of them are poking their noses round hills, others squatting in the middle of the moor and becoming diffuse ...'

Ten years on, arthritis (Joyce's and mine) starts to creak into our correspondence, and in August 1995, at a time when Roy was occupied in looking after Joyce, then only just beginning to be mobile again after a hip replacement, he had the stroke that knocked out his right arm and leg. I have two letters from the 'stupefying Gulag' of Ward 11, Macclesfield and District General Hospital, where he spent so many months. The first, telling me about the stroke and praising the methodology of the 'state-of-the-art' neuro-physiotherapists who were working to get him back on his feet, ends in mordant and get-on-with-it Fisher manner: 'No, I've not used my hospitalization to catch up with all that writing which ... No, I'm not going to write any hospital poems (why should *I* be rich and famous?) No, I've not had any profound thoughts about my condition, eternity, etcetera. A further millimetre reach on my thumb is more gratifying. Yes, I've been glad to be left-handed.'

the fisher syndrome explained

However, there was one letter of Roy's I read that was wholly unlike the rest. It dates from October 1996, not long after my first novel had been bandied about in the press as being a likely contender for the Booker-prize short-list. And as I can think of no better way to salute my fellow Geminian than by parading his talent for send-up (of me; of the whole literary-prize shenanigans), and for brilliantly sustained and inventive spoof, here it is:

After we'd talked I resolved to write to you within days on various matters arising. And now a month has passed during which I've been ceaselessly busy—with virtually nothing.

Except that one night a couple of weeks ago there reached us, well after midnight, a clamour of hoofs, distraught whinnyings, gasps and muttered imprecations. Pulling our coarse cloaks over our night attire, Dame Joyce and I hobbled out as fast as we could upon our cudgels, knowing full well that, at last, the chain we keep stretched across our deserted lane, in the hope of detaining some lost wayfarer who might bring us some profit, had yielded us a guest, albeit an unwilling one. Sure enough we espied one of heavy and powerful build, seated uneasily upon the ground and softly mouthing oaths as he pulled his knee back into joint. Meantime his steed, a fine bay, stood some way off in the moonlight, quietly cropping the grass, no whit the worse for his adventure as far as my practised eye could make out through the mist that falls from the moors above in the days after Michaelmas. The horseman cast a cold and burning eye first upon Goody Fisher who by now was swinging her cudgel to crush his pate to a pudding-mix, then upon me there as I stood appraising the likely value of his apparel and trappings. 'Slay me if you will,' he said drily in the courtly accents of the south country, 'but expect to hang from yonder tree before tomorrow sunset: for I'll be missed. My lord's men are even now on their way to double the deep word I bear to the North, lest I prove to have miscarried in some dread place such as this, and to have perished at the grimy hands of such as yon buxom crone.'

'To the North?' I queried.

'Ay, granddad, the farthest North—to Thirsk, Perth and the Wick!' he cried, 'so stint me not for the word I bear, but help me to my saddle and speed me on my way.'

'Do but tell us thy great word, and mayhap we will,' said I.

'Why, that I may,' he said evenly, 'for it can surely profit thee little in

so removed a spot. I'll tell thee as soon as I feel the soft leather of my good Cordovan saddle spread itself neath my manly parts. Come now!'

Crossing our cudgels, we lifted him up easily enough. I kept a grip on his bridle. 'The word, then!' I hissed.

He gazed haughtily, then laughed harshly. 'Why then, gaffer and goodly dame,' said he, mark it well, and ponder it well as long thou wilt, for all the good it may do thee. **'Tis naught but this: 'Rohinton Mistry for the two-thirty at Kempton Park.'**

With that he wheeled his horse and was off into the mists of the moors. Long ere his hoofbeats had vanished in his wake, my Dame and I had fallen to our knees and were giving thanks (for we had not failed to grasp the import of his contemptuously-tossed words) that **you** *were to be spared the possibly mortal embarrassment of having to sit through the Booker Prize banquet—live on TV. With hearts lighter than our limbs we helped each other to our feet and repaired to our couches, to continue with our labours of writing historical novels by candlelight beneath the counterpanes ...*

CHARLES LOCK

A Piece for Roy Fisher

A piece? Just a short thing, you understand, no more than four thousand words. Not quite an article then? An item, shall we say. Again? Another? An iteration? For us, now, not *an* item but one disarticled: *Item*. The word *item* can be either adverb or noun: where there's an article *item*'s a noun. Where not, perhaps an adverb:

Item

A bookend.

At once, the title challenges. Is this about a bookend as an item, a thing, a common noun, the commonest of such common nouns as might be considered mere items? Or is the title an adverb, signifying "likewise", "also", "same", "similar" or "next", a noting of iteration? If so, "A bookend" is one in a series, as in an inventory. In such listings *item* as adverb is still in use. As an adverb, vernacular adaptations of the Latin *idem* are commonly used in many modern languages. In those tongues we also find various nouns and verbs of sameness drawn from *idem*: identity, identify, iterate. (Note that *ibid.*, unabbreviated as *ibidem*, means "same place", as in a footnote: it is the sameness of the place that makes the item.) Only in English, however, does *idem* transform itself into a noun that floats free of the precise semantic control of *identity*. For in current English, what's an item is not expected to share an identity with another item. Idiom often retains etymological sense long after ordinary usage has abandoned it: to say about two persons "You didn't know they're an item?" (meaning, in some sense, coupled) is traced by the *OED* no further back than 1970. In that rather coy "item" the etymological sense is restored.

Without reference to identity or likeness, *item* has come to signify a "detail" or an "article", where our usage forgets (again) that both those words themselves once indicated a fragment of a whole. An item is a *detail*, that is to say part of a whole, the whole being formed by the series. Likewise, an *article* is what articulates and holds together items not identical to itself. Rabbi Klein explains: "The sense of the English noun arose from the circumstance that the word *item* was generally used to introduce all the sections of a bill, except the first."[12] Thus it is necessary to look at the first term in a series reading *item* in order to establish of what sort or kind of thing this series is made. Even if there is no more than one occurrence of "Item" we would be wise to check the preceding term in case this is a minimal series of two.

As we are now in the middle of a volume of poetry by Roy Fisher we cannot read much into the preceding item, for the order of poems is not an order for which the poet seems to have much respect. In *The Long and the Short of It: Poems 1955–2005* the preceding poem is entitled 'The Read and the Black' which of course by a well-worn pun describes any poem, any text. (Somewhat annoyingly my edition, its proofreader perhaps under the influence of Stendhal, reads 'The Red and the Black': even if we do not overlook this misprint, we are certainly free to overhear it.) Let us then assume that the poem that begins on p. 256 of *The Long and the Short of It* is not *entitled* "Item" but indicates by the adverbial '*Item*' that it carries the same title as the immediately preceding poem. There we find, in a poem published seventeen years before the one we'll know as—if not call—'Item', some play with the jargon of the inventory:

> there were crimson curtains all right,
> and cushions of the same.

Fisher is of course dedicated to the proposition that resort to sameness is an admission of failure, whether of perception or discernment. A thing is not itself from one moment to the next, in one light and another; as the angle changes, so does the thing observed. Or so, rather, does the observer, who notices things. Even the single is a fiction, a category of the incurious. For whatever's supposed to be single, identical with itself, must throw a shadow, or reflect its unlikeness, and thereby be reckoned multiple.

> I was meant to
>
> glance at it all just
> once and move on

> but I wouldn't. I fixed it.
> It tried to fix me . . .

and the poem ends with a vision of thing and reflection (the read item and its black image?) going their separate ways:

> advancing over or voyaging into
> that which is not itself ...

This may remind us of, while we also remind ourselves that it is not the same as, the crossed trajectories of visual awareness in the 'Introit' to *A Furnace*: the resistance to fixing, the defiance of all samenesses.

That bookend. One bookend assumes another, and two bookends ought not to be identical except by exhibiting mirror-image symmetry. Item, we begin to suspect, a second bookend. Or another bookend. Or even a matching bookend. But no: where "Item" is unarticled, our bookend is indefinitely articled, and solitary.

> A bookend. Consider it well
> if that's the way your mind
> runs. One-handed

Let us begin (for so my mind runs) by considering how the opening stanza takes for its limits "a bookend" and the "one-handed". The central sentence is framed by each: each, in terms of the stanza, a fragment. And each nominal fragment assumes a corresponding item with which it would form a pair. Like a hand, a bookend is an object, a thing, an item, that is not autonomous or self-sufficient, but needs to be doubled to be made one, and whole.

The opening stanza is iconically symmetrical: the nominal phrase at beginning and end: obviously incomplete at the end, but less obviously incomplete at the beginning if we read "A bookend" as syntactically linked to 'Item' with an invisible implicit colon: "Item: A bookend". "One-handed" will not find the object it would modify until another five lines have been read, and we have reached the third stanza. Thus the opening stanza is iconically stable and balanced, while syntactically it's grasping for leverage, as a one-handed person might be particularly in need of a handhold. The poem is about the difficulties of balance, metrically, arithmetically, aesthetically. One bookend invokes, calls upon its pair, and it will be done here in a three-line stanza that never reaches its own closure. Of these stanzas there are three to the power of three, or twenty-seven. Thus the total number of lines is 81, or "three to the power of four". (That in *The Long and the Short of It* the poem should begin on page "two to the power of eight" is a special treat.) Of these twenty-seven stanzas, not one is syntactically self-contained. Apart from the final stanza, only one is closed by a full stop. Of the eighty-one lines, hardly a single one is comfortably occupied and filled out by a sentence, clause or phrase. Nor is one of its lines divided around a caesura, or into matching hemistichs.

To move a thing, we rely on all our four limbs. The one-handed speaker is also lame, and cannot shift the bookend. Where it is,

> it unbalances
>
> one of the unsafe heaps that
> make up my workroom, even I
> get driven to consider it,

Thus "one-handed" modifies not the speaker but "even I" who, by the precariousness with which the bookend is balanced, gets "driven to consider" what the reader has already been urged, even commanded to consider. Such considerations bring both reader and speaker to the recognition that

> It's one of a couple. The other's long
>
> lost in the house and has turned to pure
> thought.

At once, a sublime balance of balance and imbalance. One bookend is here, to be seen; the other is not. Yet the reader is teased by the difference between the nothing that is not here and the nothing that is. Both bookends belong, for the reader, to "pure thought". Yet one is just that, and out of sight, the other is this:

the fisher syndrome explained

This one's material,

To think of a pair of things is to think of a whole. One of a pair is less than a whole. To have lost one is to be made intensely aware of the materiality of the one that remains, for it has now acquired an obdurate unclassifiable thinginess.

There's one important condition of pairs that need to be matched: one "half" cannot be substituted for another. Such a pair is made up of complementary though unlike parts. Sorting the laundry is instructive: a sock is lost until its pair is found. And a single sock is in distress. Unless, that is, all one's socks are of the same size and colour, in which case one sock can be substituted for another, and distress can be somewhat alleviated. This may also be the case with mittens, but never with gloves, or shoes. A right glove cannot take the place of a left glove. And a single glove, or shoe, or unmatched sock, loses its place and its function: utility and purpose are suspended. It no longer has a place or knows its place. In its place, one sock belongs with another, in the place where all pairs of socks belong. A single sock does not belong in such a place, nor in any of the places, conceptually or physically, to which we consign the used and useful objects of our daily lives. The one becomes just a thing, which is to say some-thing that demands our thinking, that resists our classificatory dispositions. Yet this is not just a thing like other things: a single thing for which we have no purpose can be thrown away. This one, however, is not "one" in itself, for it remains in a state of potential redemption: the other one might at any time and in any place "turn up". And if the other one does, it will only increase our frustration if in the meantime this first one has been thrown out, has become "that one I should have kept". This is a domestic dilemma which has tormented millions: yet the dilemma might itself find some redemption in the recognition of its literary implications: one throws down the gauntlet, and its pair will be proof of the challenger's identity, not unlike the way a contract works by an indenture, the rough tearing of the document producing a uniquely matching set. And a lady can solicit its return, and confirm ownership, and collusion, by producing its pair, when she cunningly lets fall her glove. Or, however unwittingly, her slipper.

And the problem has led to a philosophical problem first identified by Kant, who could not accept that all physical bodies occupy space in the same way: yet the uniform extension of space would seem to rely on the uniformity of the mode in which it could be occupied. The existence of one glove implies another, and thus sets up a contract within and across space, anticipating what nuclear physicists would later term "quantum entanglement". What these pairs share is the like-unlikeness of each member of the set: the right-left pairing, of gloves or shoes, was first given philosophical definition by Kant as "incongruent counterparts".[3] Edward Casey writes of "Kant's uncovering of the enormous consequences entailed by a tiny and almost literally invisible detail, that of right versus left hands regarded as enantiomorphic."[4]

Kant's fascination with the problem has endured. In *The Truth in Painting* Jacques Derrida considers the dispute over Van Gogh's depiction of a pair of shoes. Meyer Schapiro found much to disagree with in Heidegger's essay on Van Gogh, yet Derrida reasonably protests against their shared assumption that two shoes painted within the same frame must constitute a pair:

> A pair of shoes is more easily treated as a *utility* than a single shoe or two shoes which aren't a pair. The pair inhibits ... the "fetishizing" movement; it rivets things to use, to "normal" use; it shoes better and makes things walk according to the law. It is perhaps in order to exclude the question of a certain uselessness, or of a so-called perverse usage, that Heidegger and Schapiro denied themselves the slightest doubt as to the parity or pairedness of these two shoes.[5]

This passage is cited in an essay 'Fetishizing the Glove'[6] which investigates the use of pairs in inhibiting fetish value: Derrida himself contrasts Van Gogh's paintings of shoes with Magritte's, one of which, a single lady's shoe (or a lady's single shoe; for fetishistic purposes it may be important for the lady to be as single as the shoe) is entitled within the pictorial field 'la lune' and, outside it, 'The Key of Dreams'. Their summary is just, yet their conclusion is oddly naive:

the fisher syndrome explained

> If, as Derrida suggests, the fetish emerges when the unpaired object is no longer bound "to 'normal' use", the paradox of the single glove in the Renaissance is that it is the norm, at least within literary and artistic representations . . . the single glove was haunted by its absent other . . .[7]

To which one must respond that of course the single glove is the norm of representation, for it presents itself as a thing, an object, a problem, and as the subject of a narrative—"whether that [absent] glove was with a lover or a messenger". A narrative is not itself a sufficient condition for fetishization.

A bookend need not be a fetish, and we should look carefully at the relation between the fetishistic and the aesthetic. For the aesthetic is by Kant's definition "useless", and we need not dissent from Heidegger in his interest in the pictorial rendering of shoes as the making useless of otherwise useful objects. We might think of a fetish not as an object of sexual perversion or of an irrational obsession or devotion, but simply as a thing that, though of no use, remains of importance to us, but for reasons that are not aesthetic. The *OED* makes a pertinent clarification: a *fetish* "differs from an idol in that it is worshipped in its own character, not as the image, symbol, or occasional residence of a deity." In quotidian terms, innocent of perversion or pathology, that might be regarded as the difference between a thing that represents another (often a person: a photograph, for example) and a thing that we value for itself, without reference to anything or anyone else. The former is an idol; however absurd it may seem to use such a word of a photo depicting a child or partner, we should recognize that only in cultures that have inherited the contra-iconoclastic approval of images have painting and photography been able to flourish. We can see at once how (unlike the idol) the fetish might be mistaken for the aesthetic. To admire a portrait because it reminds us of the person depicted is to fall short of the aesthetic, in a way we might term idolatrous. To retain a thing for its own sake is also to disclaim the aesthetic. Yet both of these motives for valuing and keeping a thing disregard purpose or function. What distinguishes a thing one keeps for its own sake is that it never is quite that: a reason for discarding an object is usually phrased in terms such as this: "I don't even remember where it came from". It is the memory of its provenance that (minimally) confers value on an object: "its own sake" is actually its provenance. An heirloom is named as being treasured for its provenance, but provenance covers any narrative that tells us not about the object in itself but about the story of how it came into a particular possession.

David Jones in 'Art and Sacrament' would modify the Kantian idea of the intransitivity of art, protesting that all art is materially embodied and therefore must also act transitively on the physical world: the beauty of, say, a door-handle involves "a passing over to an object, so a transitivity."[8] Non-functional making (the "fine arts") is usually representative, so for Jones, a sculpture involves a passing over to the idea of what it represents. Implying the link between art and article, Jones write that art is etymologically a fitting together: "When we say of so-and-so that 'he perfected that work' we mean always that someone has . . . fitted certain things together. It is the fitting together that we praise."[9] Fitting together is central both to the act of making and to the deed of caring, or curating. The one is aesthetic; the other may not be aesthetic but owns no function beyond that of care: it is the fitting together of the object and what defines and explains it. A book is easily curated: its provenance can be written on its pages, or tipped in or otherwise inserted so as to be contained within it. Vases and jugs may be found on close (even intrusive) inspection to hold within their throats or necks papers declaring provenance, or proof of purchase, or attribution. A thing and its label need to be, somehow, articulated.

Thomas Hardy's poem 'The Little Old Table' declares the border between the fetish and the aesthetic, for the value here is not of aspect but of association:

> Creak, little wood thing, creak,
> When I touch you with elbow or knee;
> That is the way you speak
> Of one who gave you to me!
>
> You, little table, she brought—
> Brought me with her own hand,
> As she looked at me with a thought
> That I did not understand.

the fisher syndrome explained

      —Whoever owns it anon,
      And hears it, will never know
      What a history hangs upon
      This creak from long ago.

—except, we must consider, that the table now forms part of the Thomas Hardy Memorial Collection on display in the Dorset County Museum, and resting on the table is a copy of this poem, whose claim is thus quite brazenly falsified. Yet though we now know the table's history, nobody hears its creak.

Other objects do not lend themselves so conveniently as containers or for display of records of provenance. While some of those of enantiomorphic shape (gloves or shoes) can serve as containers, not all do.

The term "enantiomorphic" had been coined in 1856 by a crystallographer. Enantiomorphic growth is a feature of crystals, as of other natural formations, such as the snail shell or the helix. The *OED* cites an early and helpful use of enantiomorph from the *Encyclopedia Britannica* in 1885: "Two figures or two portions of matter are said to be enantiomorph to each other when these forms are not superposable, i.e., the one will not fit into a mould which fits the other, but the one is identical in form with the mirror-image of the other . . . we may take our two hands, which will not fit the same mould or glove, but the one of which resembles in figure the mirror-image of the other."

This is the figure by which we are asked to understand the behaviour of sub-atomic particles which, even when distant from each other, are yet "entangled". When quantum physicists attempt to explain the phenomenon they use the figure of gloves in two boxes, which must form a pair even though the determination of each is unknown to the other. This is the notion of "non-local connection" or "quantum entanglement" that Einstein termed "*spukhafte Fernwirkung*" or "spooky action at a distance". If one particle "decides" to go one way, the other particle must simultaneously decide to go the other; they act, over any distance, as what Kant had called "incongruent counterparts". It is happily not our task to understand quantum entanglement, but the quality of distance has its value for us: a single sock or glove is acted upon by its incongruent counterpart of whose location we have no idea. Rather, it is precisely because we have no idea; because the two gloves or socks are not in proximity, that the one we know presents itself as evidence of an incongruent counterpart elsewhere.

The double helix is the most intricate evidence of enantiomorphosis in biology: in 'Roy Fisher on Location' John Kerrigan has noted the link between the structure of DNA and the double spiral that structures *A Furnace*.[10] Fisher's most ambitious poem begins with light "crossing from the left" and closes with snails and spirals. The 'Introit' shows us

>the great iron
>thing, the ironworks,

which brings us back to our item, our enantiomorphic bookend. We should note that one book-end can be used on its own, if at the other end of the shelf is a wall. But this one seems to be good only for unbalancing:

>It's one of a couple. The other's long
>
>lost in the house and has turned to pure
>thought.

And has it thereby teased us out of thought? For the contrast between the "pure thought" of the missing bookend and the "impure thought" (?) of the unmissing one sets up an antithesis in negation that goes beyond the logic of ekphrasis. For ekphrasis celebrates in words what's visually absent, gives words to a "silent form" (such as a grecian urn) and by those words recuperates the image in the "impure thought" of what's rightly termed imagination. (Imagination is made of pictures rather than of words: such is the contractual logic of ekphrasis: there's no special term for—nor much interest in—visual renderings of words, depictions of descriptions (say, or see: the Bible Illustrated, or an Illustrated Shakespeare, or the film of the book). But look inward at what these words give shape to:

>This one's material,
>cut from three-quarter-inch softwood,

the fisher syndrome explained

> deep-stained as oak and varnished
> heavily; a few scratches. Made up
> of three pieces. The face,
>
> five inches across by four-and-three-quarters
> with the corners cut in at forty-five
> degrees from three inches up; two
>
> nails struck through to the base,
> same shape, but three by three-and-a-half,
> hollowed and plugged with lead. A buttress
>
> effective as a brick would be
> but with less style. No trace
> of commercial fancy anywhere on it.

Its material shape is measurable, though it has less style than a brick: whatever value this object has, it is not aesthetic. Its silent form provokes as words only numbers written out, their hyphens like the nails that fit the three pieces together.

Not for its aspect then, its "observable properties", but for its associations, as Hardy had noted in 1877: "the beauty of association is entirely superior to the beauty of aspect, and a beloved relative's old battered tankard to the finest Greek vase."[11] Hardy ascribes beauty to both, suggesting (if we recall David Jones) that the fitting together by aspect involves the transitivity to some shapeliness, whereas the fitting together by association involves the connection between a thing and the story about it.

> When my life's props come to suffer dispersal
> this piece gets dumped, if I've not
> done it myself first. Should it get to junk-stall
>
> there'd be nothing to know but these
> its observable properties. All the same
> it does have unshakeable provenance—unless I

> choose to suppress it. I don't.
> I've certain knowledge the thing is fifty-two
> years old, manufactured in 1944
>
> at the enormous works of the Birmingham
> Railway Carriage and Wagon Company,
> the neighbourhood's mother-ship and provider ....

In tracing this history it is suggested that "Mikhail Gorbachev would be good casting" for the foreman coach-builder who had a sideline in bookends, "when this poem's filmed". The absurdity of the casting is dwarfed by that of this poem (or any) being filmed, for that would be the reversal of ekphrasis: "You've read 'The Faerie Queene' / 'Paradise Lost' / 'The Waste Land': now see the movie!" Ekphrasis adds; for words can always supplement what is not in words. But what is not in words can seldom add much to words.

Not even this bookend: its material presence would add nothing materially to this poem. A table displayed so as not to creak (thus silencing "the way you speak") contributes nothing to Hardy's poem, and to be seriously curious about the original of Keats's Grecian urn is—in its idolatry of silent form—to turn a deaf ear to poetry. Let us hope that "A bookend" is not displayed in the Roy Fisher Memorial Collection. For a poem is its own provenance, and ekphrasis renders superfluous the materiality of that which it describes. Enantiomorphically, the entanglement involves not only the other of the pair, but the words, the account that each silent form might, by way of alibi or explanation, give to the other. When it is a poet who supplies the words, the pair can retire, both as good as lost, both

> turned to pure
> thought.

A better essayist could have fitted together a full account of Roy Fisher's poem with and into four thousand words. A poem called 'Item', an essay called 'A Piece': each might have its incongruent counterpart elsewhere. One could insist that black marks disposed on a page call out (materially) for others, elsewhere, to res pond, fittingly if incongruently.

Given that, this piece might be redeemed as a tangled salutation: both wave and article.

Notes

1. Ernest Klein, *Comprehensive Etymological Dictionary of the English Language* (s.v. item). (Amsterdam: Elsevier, 1971).
2. Tarset, Northumberland: Bloodaxe Books, 2005.
3. Edward S. Casey, *The Fate of Place: A Philosophical History*. (Chicago: University of Chicago Press, 1997), pp.205–6.
4. ibidem, p. 240.
5. Jacques Derrida, *The Truth in Painting*, tr. G. Bennington and I. McLeod. (Chicago: University of Chicago Press, 1997), pp.332–3.
6. Peter Stallybrass and Ann Rosalind Jones, 'Fetishizing the Glove' in *Things*, ed. Bill Brown. (Chicago: University of Chicago Press, 2004), pp. 174–92.
7. ibidem, pp. 191–2.
8. David Jones, *Epoch and Artist: Selected Writings*. (London: Faber, 1973), p.152.
9. ibidem, p.151.
10. John Kerrigan, 'Roy Fisher on Location' in *The Thing about Roy Fisher*, ed. John Kerrigan and Peter Robinson. (Liverpool: Liverpool University Press, 2000), p.40.
11. Michael Millgate (ed.), *The Life and Work of Thomas Hardy*, (London: Macmillan, 1984), p.124.

PETER MAKIN

The Hardness of Edges

When the total contents of each micro-package of similar wavelength reaching me distinctly (from this leaf, or from that greenhouse window-pane) are evenly diffused over the whole surface of the retina, then I can no longer see; I am effectively blind. This can be achieved (a) by placing a ground-glass plate before the face, (b) by cataract.

We depend absolutely on the distinction of this from that; our lives depend on it.

When two entities merge, they may lose the coherence that made them entities. Thus, at the dissolving border between two towns, in Roy Fisher's poem 'The House on the Border'

> Far from their centres
> two edges fuse, and backfill
> the meadows that were between, levelling
> dips, culverting streams, the streets
> facing only inwards, walls closed on
> bony bodies with soft skin, short
> hasty bodies signed with unique hair

—and the level of life falls low, like slack curtains:

> The rooms hang
> straight and dinner has turned out
> to be restrained moist white
> bread with firm cheese chunks
> that carry a whiff and a kick. Nothing
> to do but get it down, finish the day.

For 'to live is to differentiate oneself', as Rémy de Gourmont (I think) once wrote.

Then why or how do Roy Fisher's poems make us take such delight in the crumbling of barriers between this and that, between this type of thing and that? There is gusto for the list tumultuous: ". . . brick-ends, oil-cans, glints of declining /sun on tea-set gilding . . ." These are the sons of time in 'The Dow Low Drop':

the fisher syndrome explained

> When it puckers and punctures it slits . . .
>   Almost
> everything that tumbles out
> is furniture and the like, lived with
> but not digested: sideboard,
> ironing tackle, things for the kitchen
> that match, air-fresheners, seersucker
> sheets, candlewick covers,
> mugs that match, all
> the colours of crispbread; oldish
> damp towels, heaters, the mail . . .

The drollery is in the incongruity: these things that seem reasonable in their places look foolish as mates in this headlong river. Literary antecedents of this are in Bunting's trash-can in 'Narciss, my numerous cancellations prefer . . .':

>   amongst the peel
> tobacco-ash and ends spittoon lickings litter
> of labels dry corks breakages and a great deal
>
> of miscellaneous garbage picked over by
> covetous dustmen . . .

and perhaps also in Pound's 'Canto XXXIV', for the gusto is the same: "Oils, beasts, grasses, petrifactions, birds, incrustations ...". It can be associated with a hellish energy, in Fisher's interviews, that refer to Smethwick: "chimney stacks, black and rusting factory buildings, huge gasholders, a pandemonium of metallic noise, a network of oily, green canals."

 But generally the energy of the verse derives from the irony: "these things you have tried to keep in their orderly places, in their categories; but they won't stay." 'The Burning Graves at Netherton' notes what happens to a normal English churchyard when the earth it is of becomes unstable, with a slow fire gnawing the coal-seams below. That which should be separate tumbles together:

> And the gravestones
> keeled, slid out of line,
> lifted a corner, lost
> a slab, surrendered
> their design; caved
> in

There is "No cataclysm. Rather / a loss of face, a great / untidiness and shame". And we chuckle. Why?

The answer must be that we are aware of a common desire to heighten the ordered-ness of things, and that the original ordered-ness of the junk thus set drolly tumbling, being at least partly a result of that desire, had been at least partly fake. Yet demarcation exists and life cannot exist without it; Fisher's poems are what they are because of the fineness of their notation of it. I suspect that these points are the opposite ends of a tension in Fisher's mind, felt so fully that neither can overcome; so that this tension is one in which his mind is perpetually held, and without which a good part of his poetry would not have been written. (Bunting: "We write about these things because we cannot resolve them.")

And I think here we arrive at the fundamental interest or tension that energizes what Roy Fisher calls "my long file of cemetery pieces": his numerous poems about funerals, and about death and its rites in general. They relate to merging, to loss of distinction.

In death, we fear merging. We fear that we don't really know who Sally was; that if she only exists henceforth under the wing of what Bunting called that "persistent liar" memory, she will mutate; that our mutating versions of Sally probably already disagree. In that sense we are afraid of losing her. She will diffuse into the soup of the unknowable.

Hence the haste to fix on an Agreed Version of her, in the lay preacher's discourse at the funeral, which, if he is skilled enough to make us admire him and go away feeling comfortable, will be an acceptable mix of unacknowledged Types, borrowed from public discourse, "personalized" by a few slightly tuned-up anecdotes offered by her friends. "She was a woman, take her for all in all ..." Yes, that is what she was, isn't it.

the fisher syndrome explained

Hence also the haste to fix the material bits of her that remain. We have to agree what they are: this flesh (but not those false teeth), these particular bones (we don't have room for all of them), these ashes ... it is unfortunate that, as Fisher's poem 'They Come Home' carefully observes, no care can ultimately preserve some particles of the Deceased from shooting up the same municipal incinerator as the rest of the household garbage and ending up as part of the same fine haze over the North Sea. Transcending all that materiality? No; coming down somewhere over Cumbria, it may be, and ending in the organic goat's milk that ends in my poor stomach, or yours, on its way to somewhere else: "By no means separate / from anything at all." We cannot keep the dead distinct.

The poetry of Roy Fisher takes abundant delight in the contradictions that arise from this great communal effort to keep the dead fixed and separate. The flesh that we are (left for a week or two) is not greatly dissimilar from dog-food, and the rites of the Malagasies happily acknowledge this reality. They take their well-ripe dead out of the tombs and walk them round to celebrate them:

> *From the grave-clothes*
> *they fall in gobbets as dog-food*
> *falls from the can. We wrap them*
> *in fresh dry linen. They*
> *bless our lives with their happiness.*

And the poet brings this a little nearer home by postulating a similar rite, in more ancient periods, in his own valley:

> Walk them around the valley. Drop
> here a finger
> for the god that is a rat or a raven
> here a metatarsal
> to set under the hearth for luck.

Finally, there is the monument. On one occasion when I talked to Roy Fisher, he was recalling a visit to Sharrow Vale Cemetery, in Sheffield: a glory of the Victorian cemetery-maker's art. Fisher observed that the tombs were not yet much more than a hundred years old, and already at odd angles, with split marble, possibly un-rescue-able.

The tomb-makers in such a place have done their best to take the dead away from the world of the merely defective and changeable. A tomb must be not just any old heap of stones picked up in a field: it will be a smooth machine-ground granite house, twelve feet high, with in-cut letters, and with marble simulacra of other items already elevated into the categories of the eternal—angels, books, super-flowers. And if the apprentice mis-chooses the stone, and works on a piece with a flaw in it, so that the corner breaks off, that piece will not go into the monument. It is not square enough: not regular enough, not sufficiently reminiscent of the Permanent, which is regularly ordered. And if natural cataclysms occur, skewing the tombstones out of line, we feel offended.

This brings us back to the order of rhetoric, which (in more concentrated forms) is the order of poetry. The Deceased will be elevated into the permanent, at her funeral, with patterned speech, spiced here and there with pieces of poetry: words in 'straight lines', or at least lines straighter than those found in natural language, with the quasi-regular shapes formed by all the semantic and non-semantic patternings that we expect in the special utterance that is verse.

And why is all this funny? Why is it funny to have Poldy Bloom upturning it all, musing upon the poor soul who must return to the graveyard at Judgement Day, "mousing around for his liver and lights"? I think because some part of us always knows that all this dignity of placed-ness, of certainty of position, doesn't hold up.

We know, when we think about it, that so much of the assertion of identity-by-distinctness is habitual cheating.

Such heightenings of contrast occur very widely. Think, for example, of the "identity" that is in one's culture and its tongue. Roy Fisher at a certain point did a good deal of what appeared to be apologizing for the fact that his culture and its tongue were in effect a "house on the border." He seemed to regret not coming from a self-existent area, like Basil Bunting (his example), and not having a hard-edged language. His Midlands, in pronunciation and usage, was "a region of perpetual muffled fighting, a borderland between the embattled North and the complacent South." The "bland English tongue" that "I had to write

the fisher syndrome explained

---

in" he thought "pallid and limp in its sounds and its structures"; a mouthful, one might say, of the "restrained moist white / bread with firm cheese chunks" that is the cultural pap of houses on borders.

These remarks were only a sort of defensive exploration of the problem, as the careful reader of the same interviews will see; but they bring to mind some of the identity claiming by difference heightening that went on among Roy Fisher's elders and contemporaries.

Any second-rate local-colour artist plies his trade by heightening local differences. He's afraid the cosmopolitan audience might not notice them. Since the 1760s, if not earlier, WASP Englishmen and Americans have felt their culture to be 'too middle', and have attempted to escape into the more wildly different (as by them depicted) identities of Scotsmen, or of Indians—the noble Indians in question often in fact being revised versions of characters in the 'Celtic' 'epic' of Ossian. Oscar Wilde got his first name from a character in Ossian, one of the first great products of the 'fakelore' industry. My own middle-class Sheffield forebears contrived to have us descended from the MacIans, who (we were told) were gloriously massacred at Glencoe. The local colour of the wild Highlanders, much favoured by Queen Victoria, was heightened by the systematization of the clan tartans, as invented by a manufacturer in Lancashire. And some of Hugh MacDiarmid's work seems to belong to this tendency.

By birth MacDiarmid did not speak Gaelic, but Scots, linguistically a close relative of English; in fact, he spoke a dialect of Scots which was itself further attenuated in the direction of English. This was natural, since he was a Lowlander, a man of the Borders. But that was tough for a man who wanted to mark out a cultural identity that (if possible) had not been assimilated to the English power-centres at all. So he set to work with the dictionary: Jamieson's *Etymological Dictionary of the Scottish Language*.

His first published piece of Scots prose is "filled with obsolete or obsolescent Scots words" all taken from Jamieson's dictionary, "the great majority of which begin with the first three letters of the alphabet." (So Kenneth Buthlay informs us.) This was a short way to a new cultural identity. The poem 'Water Music' is mainly from Jamieson's A, B and C, supplemented, this time, from his Q, R and S.

But as a process of 'acquiring a tongue' this is very suspect. It is extremely hard properly to articulate at the level of poetry a learned (second) language: we are all familiar with slightly daft poems produced by foreigners. To the ear of a real native speaker, a string of semantic near misses will somehow betray itself. None of this affects the power of these poems for me, since I am not a native speaker of broad Scots (still less of the broad Scots that was spoken when these words from Jamieson were last used in action). But as the marking out of a different cultural identity, which ought to amount to a subtly different form of life, it has about the same value as Poe's taking on a sailor's identity in the language of *The Narrative of Arthur Gordon Pym*, of Forrest Carter's taking on the language of a half-Cherokee boy in *The Education of Little Tree,* or of the 1970s scriptwriter Ned Perry's taking on the poetic cadences of a mid-19th century West-Coast chief in 'Chief Seattle's Thoughts', soon to be tacked up on the walls of a thousand American schoolrooms as inspirational Native dicta on ecology. All fakelore: all the work of middle-WASPS trying to be colourfully different, trying to be un-middle.

Bunting, who was on Fisher's mind when he muttered quasi-defensively about his own language, kept his urge to be un-English more under control. The Northumbrianisms that he uses are, I think, mainly ones he had heard in action. But even for him there could be contrivance in this heightening of difference. At certain points he decided that *Briggflatts* should be delivered in the Northumbrian tongue, most particularly with its peculiar /r/. But in performance, after a while, he would forget this point, as he became absorbed in the matter of the poem, and drift back to the RP /r/. The Northumbrian rhotacism was not native to him. Swinburne, in some ways Bunting's model, was more expert: his 'ballads of the English border' are masterpieces of archaeological consistency—like the medieval church in my village that was rebuilt by Sir Giles Gilbert Scott. And one does not mistake these for the real thing.

The heightening of differences, the maintaining of them, the arranging of entities into repeats = patterns = order, as claims on a stable place in time/space and therefore identity: these are all very fundamental human activities, and probably always teetering on the border between what is necessitated and what is only self-delusion perpetrated for the purpose of comfort.

the fisher syndrome explained

But there remains what is in itself different, though, it may be, with a low-key difference. The greater realism or honesty is to accept it, as it is, without heightening, which is difficult, because it often requires more acute acts of perception.

'Top Down, Bottom Up' describes the slow murder of a tree by a pair of busy young goats. Death progresses slowly and irreversibly, as they obliviously chew their way through the tree's means of life. It's a sort of comedy of indignity; a perfectly natural process, showing the disorder built into the way things are. But there are two main elements in tension. Setting them up in such a way that the reader will feel the tension between them requires the utmost exactitude of observation—that is, of distinction. There is the tree, which has to be presented anthropomorphically:

> The old tree, dying already from the top,
> dies faster, with bolder strokes
> that take whole branches out
> to hang hooked up and bare to the sky
>
> when all the others tip their fresh
> leaves down by handfuls and lift
> blossom-cones through the shade.
>
> What's living rises by sinuous
> rivers of lichened bark, inaccessibly
> turned in the complex trunk . . .

But the greater attention is paid to the goats, their postures, and the forms of their wounds:

> erect on stretched hindlegs, throats
> vertical, mouths upthrust, the pious
> and guilty eyes oblique in their heads
> as they ate the tree,
>
> baring the white wood
> to the curve of a back
> patterned with progressed teethmarks

Visually this has the precision that makes a metaphor work. "Pious / and guilty eyes" gives the bigness of goats' eyes as well as their slottiness, in such a way that one can read over them the human eyes with the attitudes Fisher wishes us to infer. "To the curve of a back" evokes the body-ness of some odalisque by Ingres, and "patterned with progressed teethmarks" brings up the physicality of this process, with a visual presence that prevents the whole thing from being mere projected lament. This is a body, being chewed. There must be a quasi-physical sense of pain; there must be a sense of the agents' self-absorbed irresponsibility:

> nibbling a tidy edge to the wound
> and quietly subsiding with straight stares
> through distant eye-slots.

One cannot have these without what those old literalists Pound and Bunting would have called "precise observation of things", which is to say precise observation of pre-existent differences. Not every poet can handle this, and the poets with the most striking 'local colour' are not necessarily the ones who can give us their world.

And of course it doesn't require an interestingly different language: only a vast lexical range, a great variety of syntactic nuances, an ear for the social registers, and the rest of what is at the disposal of a master of one of the great *koine*.

Distinctions are always there, in the universe as we know it so far; when some major structure is degraded and merges with what surrounds it, at a micro-level there still remain distinctions between structures, to be observed, to be compared. So the collapse of major structures like trees does not imply loss of differences.

Does Roy Fisher believe this? I don't know. There is so much in his writing that celebrates the folly of asserting distinctions. No one is more aware than he of the fluidity of language, for example. In 'Irreversible' he makes fun of the hero of *Briggflatts*, who castigates himself thus for weaknesses of character that make him write shoddily and therefore transiently:

the fisher syndrome explained

>Name and date
>split in soft slate
>a few months obliterate.
>
>Wind writes in foam on the sea

—which implies clearly that if one's character weren't weak one could write in a language like granite. There is no such language, says Fisher's poem; language is inherently unstable:

>Chisellers! cut deep
>into the firm, glistening
>sand—
>
>*Norseman, pass by!*

With this (and with the joke at the expense of Yeats's stoic defiance of time) we are brought back to the world of Fisher's wobbly tombstones.

Thus, once again, in his most recent long poem, 'The Dow Low Drop', a bronze-age chieftain has been buried—on a ridge overlooking the valley that Fisher the poet lives in—with all ceremony and apparatus of continuity:

>>With these things and others
>they placed my own dead body that I had
>
>to be food for the journey
>all rivets and the like must make.
>
>Under the floor I could feel the deep
>spindle of rock within the ridge of rock
>narrowly holding us up for ever.

Mother Earth has a raying-out of deep spokes that link us—or a chieftain in a mound, buried tight to her bosom—safely to Her sure Centre. But the odd consequences of things, for which the Fisherian nose has an acute flair, rule otherwise. In this case it turned out that the twentieth century required the particular stone of the ridge to manufacture toothpaste, and so it was cut out from under him:

> The whole ridge
> went. The pillar went
> as I went. The rivets, saved.

Not so surprising, either, that the rivets were saved. In the poem's view (if we read carefully) the grave-goods had not been equipment for the journeying spirit-in-its-material-body: they had set forth together on the journey that "all rivets and the like must make." Rivets, bodies, grooved bronze daggers, metric kilotonnes of slacked lime, all in democratic disorder down time's river. That for the eternal distinctness of a great chieftain in death.

In a great deal of Fisher's poetry it appears that things cannot be known because of the lies of perception. It may also be that they cannot be known because of their inherent fluidity, which, if taken at its word, means inherent non-distinct-ness. One could ask why, given that he is so concerned with the unknowableness of what is out there, he is also so concerned with establishing particular historical (biological, ecological, linguistic) facts and their interrelations. The answer might be an epistemology that amounts to a relativity of hunches: you compare two probables, using all the (necessarily unreliable) data you can find, and choose the greater. To me that would be a valid pragmatic answer, of the kind we live by; but, in a given sensibility, it may leave unsatisfied a tension between two great magnetic poles (distinctness of identity; crumbling into unknowable soup), each of which fascinates and lures like Moreau's Sphinx.

To survive, we depend on distinguishing things. Visually, this cannot take place without focus; and focusing is done by comparing levels of contrast. The eye-muscle changes the focal length until it finds the point at which the contrast-levels of the image are highest. It turns out that contrast is crucial to our existence. No wonder we hype it up.

But when our photos are a bit blurred (from bad focus, or an unstable camera), we apply the relevant software and heighten contrast. The software operates by joining up groups of same-tone pixels. It adds to adjacent blacks until they make one clearly outlined dot, and

the fisher syndrome explained

---

suppresses 'stray' blacks that are outside that. It does this irrespective of the shape of the scene originally photographed. It is inherently a falsification: like the heightening of contrasts in the lay-preacher's eulogy, or in W. H. Auden's smart little funeral poems.

I would like to think that Fisher's position stands on mysterious demarcations that are so low-contrast as to be almost imperceptible:

> If I didn't dislike
> mentioning works of art
>
> I could say
> the poem has always
> already started, the parapet
> snaking away, its grey line guarding
> the football field and the sea
>
> —the parapet
> has always already started
> snaking away, its grey line
> guarding the football field and the sea

Like the subtle line between sea and land that Whitman claimed was a starting-point for his whole vision:

> Even as a boy, I had the fancy, the wish, to write a piece, perhaps a poem, about the sea-shore—that suggesting, dividing line, contact, junction, the solid marrying the liquid—that curious, lurking something, (as doubtless every objective form finally becomes to the subjective spirit,) which means far more than its mere first sight, grand as that is—blending the real and the ideal, and each made portion of the other . . .

But I don't know.

RALPH PITE

Roy Fisher's Waterways

"There's a law // dirt grows out of" ('Abstracted Water')[1]

Birmingham developed out of the canal system. Between 1768 and 1772, "the Birmingham Canal" linked Birmingham and Wolverhampton and connected both to the Staffordshire and Worcestershire Canal. The route became known as "the main line" and many branches spread from it, within Birmingham, around the Black Country and northwards to Cannock and Lichfield. The network's 160 miles of waterways, known as the "Birmingham Canal Navigations", joined the city to the rest of the country and gave access to the sea, providing the transport system which the city's industrial and commercial expansion relied upon. On the main line, traffic became so heavy by the early nineteenth century that the canal was rerouted and rebuilt by Thomas Telford. Reservoirs and pumphouses were constructed across the district to supply water for the canals (rather than the population).

Traffic on the canals declined as first the railways took a greater share and later the roads. Canal historians point to the long, cold winter of 1962–63, when many routes were frozen for months, as the end of the waterways as a carrier of goods. Post-war neglect of the canals, leading to many ceasing to be navigable and many others being closed, in-filled and the land built over, has been resisted by voluntary organisations (such as the *Birmingham Canal Navigations Society*, founded in 1968) and reversed by an enormous increase in canal holidays over the last forty years.

Roy Fisher's career as a poet begins at the point when canals were perhaps at their least viable economically and their least fashionable. *City* depicts a landscape dominated by roads and once ruled by railways:

> In the century that has passed since this city has become great, it has twice laid itself out in the shape of a wheel. The ghost of the older one still lies among the spokes of the new, those dozen highways that thread constricted ways through the inner suburbs, then thrust out, twice as wide, across the housing estates and into the countryside, dragging moraines of buildings with them. Sixty or seventy years ago there were

the fisher syndrome explained

> other main roads, quite as important as these were then, but lying between their paths. ('Lullaby and Exhortation for the Unwilling Hero', *City*, *LS*, 32)

If the modern city is one road network overlaid upon an earlier one, the Victorian city had its limits and extent determined by the railway.

> A hundred years ago this was almost the edge of town. The goods yards, the gasworks and the coal stores [....] And this was as far as the railway came, at first. A great station was built, towering and stony. The sky above it was southerly. The stately approach, the long curves of wall, still remain, but the place is a goods depot with most of its doors barred ('By the Pond', *City*, *LS*, 36)

Canals seem insignificant in the successive waves of erasure and rebuild that have swept across the landscape, like the wars that "have come down the streets [...] like rainwater floods in the gutters" (*LS*, 33). Fisher discovers the lost streets which, despite being relegated and sidelined by all the rapid changes in the place, nonetheless, "By night, or on a Sunday, you can see [...] for what they are" (*LS*, 32). Similarly, the goods yard, though abandoned and empty even of ghosts, remains a "gigantic ghost of stone" that people are "too frightened" to pull down (*LS*, 36).

Canals do not feature in the poem in the same way: the only direct reference to them comes when Fisher mentions the "arrogant ponderous architecture" of the nineteenth century, "which dwarfed and terrified the people"; monuments in this style include "striding canal bridges" alongside "the thick-walled abattoir" and the "railway viaducts" (*LS*, 35–6). There are, in addition, "Wharves, the oldest parts of factories, tarred gable ends" and a pond of "pallid water / With yellow rushes crowding toward the shore" (*LS*, 35); the latter, though, are no more than fleeting glimpses of what "is bitter enough [to] serve as conscience" amidst a scene conquered by the amoral will to power. Apart from them, Fisher aligns waterways with the dominant, invasive force that built the city—canal bridges come "striding" through the Birmingham area, bearing down on it, in the same way that development covers over the river; the river that "shudders as dawn drums on its culvert" (*LS*, 36).

Clearly, Fisher's perspective on water and waterways has shifted so that, by the time of 'Texts for a Film', written in 1991—first published in *Birmingham River* (1994) as 'Six Texts for a Film'—"covered river[s]" lie at the heart of the city's underground. The "abstracted water" which supplied the canal system reveals Nature harnessed and "used". By doing so it displays once more the drive to exploit that formed the settlement; at the same time, however, water offers memories, survivals and revivals of the used.

>   Secrets
> half-guarded, absorbed; secrets forgotten
>
> left to decay, bursting apart,
> letting the dead stuff spill out.
>   (*LS*, 294)

As in *A Furnace* and *City*, Fisher finds traces of the visionary in the neglected—the charlatans, "detectable / identities, of gear-shifts, stumblings, jackets"—but here the neglected is found canal-side, rather than among the "subterranean / pea-green cafés" or on "the long plunging / high-walled walkway down / beside the railway viaduct" (*A Furnace*, 'III: Authorities', *LS*, 66, 69); similarly, Fisher focuses on canals rather than the newly-built estates and roads of 'Handsworth Liberties', where "two roads of similar importance / but different ages, join, // doubling the daylight / where the traffic doubles" (*LS*, 270).

This shift partly responds, I think, to the redevelopment of waterside districts in Birmingham (and other large industrial cities, notably Manchester and Salford) from the late nineteen eighties onwards. The Gas Street Basin was made over as a chic district of warehouse flats and boutiques; the old waterways of run-down manufacturing were subjected to Urban Renewal and regeneration. The poems appear early in that process, rather like elegies for the unloved and squalid industrial landscape whose makeover looms when, as Fisher notices, "The boat called 'Heritage' / comes dredging" ('Abstracted Water', *LS*, 294).

the fisher syndrome explained

The change of focus also allows, however, another reconsideration by Fisher of the force that shapes the city—how that force might be characterised and understood. *City* is a poem of bulldozers, demolition and flattening: "the entire place has been razed flat, dug over, and smoothed down again" (*LS*, 29). *A Furnace*, shadowed from the beginning by "the biggest of all the apparitions, / the great iron / thing, the ironworks" which "makes quiet burning / if anything at all" (*LS*, 53) depicts a city which has been forged and reforged, melted, hardened, broken up and melted down once more. Whether "anything at all" comes out of all this, and if so, what, Fisher hesitates to say. It may be only that "quiet" is made into "burning" by the process which is Birmingham (and this is felt as both the destruction of peace and quiet, and as the transformation of the quotidian into something radiant). Harm and transfiguration seem equally possible. Likewise, instead of the departing tail-lights of *City* and the lamps which "shine oddly, and at mysterious distances, as if they were in a marsh", in *A Furnace*, "The land, high and low / has been scattered across with fire-pots; / brick, iron, lidded, open to the sky, / the glare streaming upward / in currents and eddies of sparks" (*LS*, 29, 81). In this setting, metamorphosis and release come streaming out of city-lights.

Accordingly, *A Furnace* tracks Birmingham's origins back farther than the Victorian forefathers who erected the ponderous massy architecture of *City*. Where once "Brunel was welcome" (*LS*, 36) Fisher identifies "Puritan materialism", though it too, like Brunel in the earlier work, is being displaced.

> Puritan materialism dissolves its matter,
> its curdled massy acquisition; dissolves
>   the old gravity of ponderous fires
>   that bewildered the senses,
>   and for this
>   glassy metaphysical void.
>
>   (*LS*, 76)

The same contrast was cast, in *City*, in terms of deception, the modern being "the creation of salesmen rather than of engineers" and hiding beneath its twinkling eyes and fairground design the same "hard will" that the Victorians unashamedly displayed (*LS*, 36). *A Furnace* regards the difference as a more far-reaching change, from matter to void, from sensory, sublime fires to abstraction and imprisonment.

'Texts for a Film', more colloquial and in structure more relaxed and rambling than *A Furnace*, re-construes the process that made the city, using water as the dominant metaphor (rather than ponderous fires or quiet burning) and finding through that more incremental transformations and a more immediate, innate balance between contraries.

> What hand, what eye. Indeed. To have made
> a work of art that's at the same time
> the by-product of a spastic purpose,
> oozing as miraculous drops
> from a sort of spirit into a sort of matter,
> gathering in pools, trickling to fill
> wrinkles, indentations, then congealing as
> masonry: factories, floods of houses,
> shallowing as they spread, converted
> again to spirit in the understanding. Spirit
> filtered through brickwork. Counter-Nature
> caught into the sculpture and leased out
> like the Nature that drips all down
> the front of La Sagrada Familia.
>
> (*LS*, 288–9)

"What immortal hand or eye / Could frame thy fearful symmetry" from Blake's 'The Tyger' is the question Fisher asks in shorthand here— the same question that underlies much in his earlier treatments of Birmingham, always central to his writing though voiced with different degrees of explicitness and confidence at different times. The allusion evokes Blake's "burning bright" creature plus the hammer, the chain, the furnace and the anvil, all the fierce art that created the tiger's ferocity.[2] Instead of the furnaces of Los, however, or the infernal energies of the Black Country, Fisher sees spirit held in matter almost by accident, as a side-effect, unnoticed because secretive—oozing, gathering and trickling, sensuously and luxuriously, and as if the city were a limestone cave, its surfaces smoothed into extravagant pearly forms by the deposits that chalky water leaves behind. Gaudí's Cathedral of La Sagrada Familia in Barcelona is built to suggest natural architecture of this kind and the processes of accretion and congealing which construct it. The building melts and sticks like wax before your eyes; your understanding converting it from matter into spirit and back again.

Reading the city under the sign of water like this makes its creation feel like emergence: "The artist of the place / left plenty to chance, and time / and again got well served out" (*LS*, 289). Fisher allows a feeling of contentment to enter these lines, and the history of the place seems, for a while, natural (though "served out" is a phrase that might ring alarm bells). The mind's reaching after understanding is drawn into alignment with the untroubled, cyclical sequence of historical change so that the city becomes not only what Fisher, famously, "thinks with" but a channel for spirit—the places, for him, that spirit is filtered through.

The unusual ease of these lines is offset not only by "got well served out" afterwards but by similarly odd choices within them—by phrases such as "filtered through" or, in the following line, "caught into" and "leased out". Each of these is differently unsettling: spirit "filtered through" may be screened or cleansed, purified (that is, normalised); "caught into", instead of the more usual "caught in" hints at capture and petrifaction, giving a more vivid impression of the artist instinctively clutching something, unsure what it is, and in the same moment giving the sense of "Counter-Nature" held in and restrained; likewise, and most forcefully, "leased out" disappoints the pastoral wish for innocent control, bringing back into this poem the "hard will", territorial and ungiving, that Fisher has identified in Birmingham from the outset.

Elsewhere in the sequence, Fisher's poetry is shaped in the same way by a tension between a visionary impulse and an insistent honesty—a resistance to glossing over the ugliness of Birmingham's canals or ignoring the will to profit which is visible everywhere because it is the governing principle of the whole. This sceptical impulse coexists with Fisher's search for the artist of the place, for signs of spirit filtered through brickwork. Tension between the two poles is felt particularly strongly in relation to canals because they are viewed so often as country within the city, as separate from (and a relief from) the surrounding ugliness. By making canals into havens of refreshment hidden away within urban racket and sprawl, enthusiasts continue the habit of mind and feeling which dislikes urban sprawl itself and disregards it, ensuring that "Most of it has never been seen" (*LS*, 37).

L.T.C. Rolt, in *Narrowboat*, his pioneering celebration of the English waterways and those who made their living on them, first published in 1944, begins by presenting canals as an idyll we may chance upon.

> Most people know no more of the canals than they do of the old green roads which the pack-horse trains once travelled. [...] Knowledge of them is confined to the narrow hump-backed bridges which trap the incautious motorist, or to an occasional glimpse from a train of a ribbon of still water winding through the meadows to some unknown destination.[3]

This glimpse of "still water" can be found and particularly enjoyed within the built-up areas which canals helped to create.

> To step down from some busy thoroughfare on to the quiet tow-path of a canal, even in the heart of a town, is to step backward a hundred years or more and to see things in a different, and perhaps more balanced perspective. The rush of traffic on the road above seems to become the purposeless scurrying of an overturned anthill beside the unruffled calm of the water, which even the slow passage of the boats does not disturb.[4]

Present-day canal enthusiasts repeat Rolt's feeling almost precisely, delighting in the calm that the waterways offer amidst the busyness of urban life. The following is from a 2009 blog of a trip along the Tame Valley Canal, which belongs to the Birmingham Canal Navigations and runs round the northern edges of the conurbation.

> From below the only thing that set the aqueducts apart from their railway counterparts were the over thick spans built to accommodate four feet of water rather than 2ft of ballast. That and the steady drip drip drip from the many weeping

the fisher syndrome explained

---

leaks which exist.

Below, at ground level, cars dashed about in a profusion of noise and speed, making photography a dangerous sport. But up above, up about 70 steps, there was the peace and tranquillity of a pensioned off canal, populated only by a few fishermen and even fewer boaters.

It's not my favourite canal, but it is the closest to my home and it certainly isn't without merit.[5]

Rolt's book was illustrated when it first appeared, despite the constraints of war-time publishing. The most recent reprint adds a section of black and white photographs intended for the first edition and taken by Angela Rolt. Similarly, as above, canal enthusiasts are frequently photographers, so that you can find on the internet countless pictures of the English waterways, both within and beyond urban settings.[6]

The pictorial richness of canals marries with their perceived quaintness. Fisher's writing highlights instead their squalor, "flavoured with diesel, / rust, warm discharges", and their commercial origins as "venture-water" (*LS*, 294), but not doing so simply to expose the falsity of the conventional image. Fisher sees himself as being viewed, at one point, as "Helplessly judgmental", "Foul-mouthed and equable" (*LS*, 367). Accompanying the critical and argumentative habits, his writing about canals seeks also to sustain and set free the waterways' ability to help us really to "see things", as Rolt puts it, "in a different [...] perspective".

His work compels us to attend to things we might usually and willingly ignore and registers too his own wish to ignore them, to slip back "home / and in under the rooves" (*LS*, 273). Refurbishing canal-side properties is typical of that search for "comfort"; it leads us to "rebuild the house [...] forcing warmth, dryness / and windows with views into / the cottage below canal-level". Fisher is drawn to these animal and visual pleasures but remains irritated by them, dissatisfied and *un*comfortable.

> This comfort
> beckons. It won't do. It beckons.
> Driving steadily through rain in

> a watertight car with the wipers going.
> It won't do. It beckons.
>
> (*LS*, 138)

"It beckons" ticks here like the wipers going; the phrase beckoning, pulling the attention back and forth as wipers will distract a driver's intent, forward gaze, moving it crossways again and again—towards houses beside the road where you might stop, where you conjure up scenes of domestic bliss behind the glowing windows. And the dry car (where you can notice your scruples) is itself, of course, just as compromised and comfortable as the modernised cottage, just as luxuriously "watertight" and insulated.

Fisher's poem, 'Continuity' has a very similar moment when closed cars ("Faces behind car-glass painted with reflection, / pressed in the seats, warm bodies") are set against "So much free water", and where the lyricism of a natural water-course is found again in oily puddles beside a level-crossing. "There is smoke folded in the waters," Fisher concedes and insists, but:

> the fish-trap gives the waters form,
> minimal form, drawn on the current unattended,
> the lure and the check.

The rhythm of the final phrase, the lightness of its peaceful breathing, is an instance of the "minimal form" that the fish-trap's presence creates in the stream unnoticed. When a moment later the cars drive away and their "exhausts patter on the dirt / stained through with oils, sterile with gases", the tenderness of the earlier description seems to come from a vanished world. Fisher, though, immediately counteracts that impulse.

> When they pull away across the ballast
> dirty Nature claims her own.
>
> Tongues of grease in rings of light.
>
> The towns are endless as the waters are.
>
> (*LS*, 375)

The lines' forcefulness conveys Nature's determination to make her claim, her refusal to be denied or ousted. Where she is found and what she is found in are at once prosaic and difficult to describe—"Tongues of grease in rings of light".

In a similar manner, the concluding gnomic statement is perhaps less comfortable than it might first appear. A glimpse of infinity, which makes a townscape the doorway into the sublime, coincides with the sense that countryside has disappeared beneath ever expanding swathes of housing. "Country's nothing but a single island / lapped in City, a benign / fistula", as Fisher observes in 'Texts for a Film' (*LS*, 293). Fisher collocates "benign" and "fistula" so that the visceral unpleasantness of "fistula" is offset by "benign" while "benign" is given greater intensity and purity through the implied contrast with "malign", a contrast between medical terms that fistula's presence brings forward. As at the end of 'Continuity', he jars a conventional distaste for the urban ("fistula", "The towns are endless") against a language of praise ("benign", "as the waters are") that is always in danger of becoming in its own way bland and conventional.

Hence, in 'Wonders of Obligation', which Fisher places first in *The Long and the Short of It*, as if to suggest the poem might be considered a manifesto or apologia, recognition of objects is said to have "come / through obduracy / discomfort and trouble" and once recognised an object such as "the alder / concentrates my mind / to the water / under its firm green" (*LS*, 18, 19). Concentrates "to", Fisher writes, instead of "concentrates *on*". The change of preposition means that the alder becomes a lens and the mind a participant in the object, focussed by the tree and blended with the water. "Under" is unexpected in the same way, though less markedly so; "beneath" would, I think, be more usual. Coupled with "firm", "under" hints that power exists in the alder; it seems to control both water and observer through the strength of its colour. The slightness of the disturbances in Fisher's verbal texture maintains the impression of ordinary objects, which have not been made over by an entrepreneurial writer, while the presence of these oddnesses also allows his and the reader's re-cognitions to be new, revived perceptions.

'Wonders of Obligation' recognises in this way moths, hares, Lloyd's farm, "A little old woman / with a pink nose" (*LS*, 15) and assorted other things, relaying the peculiarity of each via the reader's momentary "discomfort and trouble". Water figures in this poem of gratitude to the ordinary—in, for instance, "a tangle of watery ruts / that shone between holly hedges" and "Streaks of life / awkward / showing among straw tussocks / in shallow flood" (*LS*, 17,19)—but also, in a change of tone, Fisher regrets its absence.

> I want
> to remark formally, indeed
> stiffly, though not complaining,
> that the place where I was raised
> had no longer deference for water
> and little of it showing. The Rea,
> the city's first river,
> meagre and under the streets;
> and the Tame
> wandering waste grounds,
> always behind
> some factory or fence.
>   (*LS*, 19–20)

This verse-paragraph ends with the "brook / nearest home" where "the caddis-flies would case / themselves in wondrous grit" (*LS*, 20), another occasion when Fisher wonderfully combines texture with visionary possibility. The loss of "deference", however, evokes the "polytheism without gods" of *City* and "the Mother [that] vanished from the planet's hide" of 'The Dow Low Drop' (*LS*, 26, 43). Water is endued, in other words, with a numinous quality; it is an element that deserves deference.[7]

This passage from 'Wonders of Obligation', published in 1979, foreshadows 'Birmingham River', from 'Texts for a Film', both pieces tracking the rivers on their inglorious progress through the districts, the old villages, of Birmingham: "in channels / that force them clear of the gasworks. And the Tame // gets marched out of town in the policed calm / that hangs under the long legs of the M6" (*LS*, 291). The alliteration ("Tame [...] out of town") adds to the sense of pre-emptory dismissal, while the half-rhyme of "Tame" and "calm" accentuates, among other

the fisher syndrome explained

---

things, the double meaning of the river's name, highlighting a question about being tamed, how close that is to being quashed, oppressed or forgotten. The opening of T.S. Eliot's 'The Dry Salvages' is remembered here, along with Spenser's poetry in celebration of grander English rivers such as the Thames or Severn—rivers with which the insignificant Rea and Tame can scarcely compete. Mock-epic lightens the pollution of the waters to create a rueful comedy which Fisher can then challenge. The couplet about the M6 comes three-quarters of the way through the poem and is the first since the opening lines to finish a sentence at the line-end. Hitherto, all the two-line units have run on into the next. With the consequent sense of (effortful) resumption, Fisher goes on:

> These living rivers
> turgidly watered the fields, gave
>
> drink; drove low-powered mills, shoved
> the Soho Works into motion, collected waste
>
> and foul waters. Gave way to steam

"These living rivers" is the poem's only half-line; "gave / drink" leads on to "Gave way to steam" which leads on to "Gave way / to clean Welsh water", to "Sank out of sight", to "Ceased" and "became / drains" (*LS*, 291). The last of these is the only one that does not begin a new sentence, the full-stops and the stark opening verbs suggesting a progress without current or flow, a forced decline of successive concessions likely from an element that naturally "gave" drink.

As in 'Wonders of Obligation', Fisher is unwilling to complain, in part because lament for ruined nature is such a cliché, in part because it is a convention of feeling and writing that prevents recognition of the thing ruined. Nonetheless, mourning coexists here with an energised awareness of the energy that went into suppressing these rivers and their living waters. Likewise, in 'Abstracted Water', the last of the sequence, Fisher is struck both by the ingenuity and self-confidence which abstracts water in order to make use of it and by the lack of deference for the element itself. The writing enters the mind-set of the user, mimicking the dismissive point of view which will see water as something leaking out of the hills ready to be "cornered". It is, however, from within that perspective that unexpected "secrets" emerge.

> secrets forgotten,
>
>   left to decay, bursting apart,
>   letting the dead stuff spill out. Sunlight
>
>   under bridges stays enclosed,
>   lattices to and fro. There's a law
>
>   dirt grows out of.
>
> (*LS*, 294)

The off-hand treatment of these materials, characteristic of the mind concerned only with water as "a proposition in hydraulics", a "float-medium" that "carries coal, parties, makes money" — this perspective becomes entangled in contradictions. Another law is found to be in operation, one that generates filth and one that may be generating a filth that is itself generative, and whose generativeness may, indeed, overturn "law". When the last lines reveal this possible sense, it allows a Blakean, infernal reversal of terms earlier on: the "dead stuff spilling out" may be coming back into life, as bursting apart comes to sound like a seed-pod erupting; likewise, the sunlight that "stays enclosed" may not be trapped but held, voluntarily, its movement as it "lattices to and fro" becoming another trace of the "lure and the check" of "free water". Though the forcefulness in 'Continuity' is largely muted here, Nature's obstinate persistence emerges to the same degree, her lack of deference alongside ours, as Fisher's waterway reveals the element's "Streaks of life" that are so "awkward" to us.

Notes

[1] Roy Fisher, *The Long and the Short of It: Poems 1955–2005* (Bloodaxe Books: Tarset, 2005), 294. Quotations from Fisher's poems are from this edition, unless indicated, using the abbreviation *LS*.

the fisher syndrome explained

---

2. William Blake, 'The Tyger', ll. 3–4, 13–15, *Songs of Experience* (1794), facsimile edition (New York: Dover Publications, 1984), pp. 14, 34–5.
3. L.T.C. Rolt, *Narrowboat* (1944, revised ed. 1948) (History Press: Stroud, 2009), 11.
4. Rolt, *Narrowboat*, 12. Rolt connects this step back into the past with access to "what is left to us of that older England of tradition which is fast disappearing" (*Narrowboat*, 12). This sentiment too survives. Steve Haywood, *One Man and a Narrowboat: Slowing Down Time on England's Waterways* (Chichester: Summersdale, 2009; first published 2004 as *Fruit Flies Like a Banana*) begins his journey by parodying it: "'The English soul,' I explained. 'The basis of our being, the core of our identity … I thought, erm, I might take a trip around the waterways of England … to sortta look for it …'." (p.1)
5. http://captainahabswaterytales.blogspot.com/ 'Tame Valley Canal, Sunday 5 July 2009'. Another entry reads: "Mooring just before bridge 69 was a good move. That extra half a mile and an earth bank deflected the noise from the M42, a road which drones on all night." (Hopwood to Tipton, 23 July 2009)
6. See for instance the gallery at: http://www.geograph.org.uk/gallery/canals_of_the_west_midlands_birmingham_canal_navigations_8323.
7. Fisher's sequence 'Matrix', focussed tightly on water, may be hinting at something similar through its title. *OED* gives "mater", mother, as the word's root, and "womb, uterus, ovary" as its first meaning.

IAN POPLE

Some observations on 'Experimenting'

Interiors with Various Figures was first published in 1966, in Simon Cutts' Tarasque Press edition, with no titles to the ten poems. Titles were returned to the pieces when they were collected in Fisher's various *Collected*s. The publication with no titles suggests that Fisher was keen for the poems to run into each other, to comment on and refract on each other without the 'artificial' separations of the titles. Their very title, redolent as it is of the nomenclature of painting, suggests not only the fact that there is a situation which is described and which is inside a posited 'domesticity', but that there are others who are disposed and situated within those interiors. Unusually in Fisher's oeuvre, outside *The Ship's Orchestra*, the pieces concentrate on characters in situations, and set up fictions with implied narratives. Thus they might be seen as forming a bridge in Fisher's work between the failed novel from which *City* was extracted in 1961 and 1962 and *The Ship's Orchestra*, published later in 1966. They often describe bizarre gender relationships, and dialogue between the participants is often quite surreal. As such these pieces, too, explore the boundaries between Self and Other in a way which weaves together the symbolic and the concrete with the irruption of semantic and expressive intentions that override that homeostasis of norms and expectations within these domestic interiors.

Commentators on 'the uncanny' draw attention to the fact that Freud's German title to his essay is 'Das Unheimlich', or literally 'the unhomelike'. Fisher's narrative interiors suggest domesticity, but are distinctly 'unhomelike'. Nicholas Royle also comments that the uncanny is 'bound up with a compulsion to tell, a compulsive storytelling', and these pieces have narratives but the reader seems only able to perceive them dimly below the surface of the poems. An extended reading of the first of these pieces, 'Experimenting', will show, I suggest, how the uncanny can occur in Fisher's writing. In this piece, a man and a woman are in a room.

> Experimenting, experimenting,
>   with long damp fingers twisting all the time and in the dusk
> white like unlit electric bulbs she said
> 'This green goes with this purple,' the hands going,
> the question pleased: 'Agree?'

the fisher syndrome explained

Squatting beside a dark brown armchair just round from the
    fireplace, one hand on a coal scuttle the other prickling across
    the butchered remains of my hair,
I listen to the nylon snuffle in her poking hands,
experimenting, experimenting.
'Old sexy-eyes,' is all I say.

So I have to put my face into her voice, a shiny baize-lined
    canister that says all around me, staring in:
'I've tried tonight. This place!' Experimenting. And I:
'The wind off the wall paper blows your hair bigger.'

Growing annoyed, I think, she clouds over, reminds me she's a
    guest, first time here, a comparative stranger, however close;
    'Doesn't *welcome* me.' She's not young, of course;
trying it on, though, going on about the milk bottle, tableleg,
the little things. Oh, a laugh somewhere. More words.
She knows I don't *live* here.

[…]
but she shuts her eyes big and mutters:
        'And when the moon with horror—
        And when the moon with horror—
        And when the moon with horror—'
So I say 'Comes blundering blind up the side tonight'.
She: 'We hear it bump and scrape'.
I: 'We hear it giggle'. Looks at me,
'And when the moon with horror,' she says.

Squatting beside a dark brown armchair just round from the
    fireplace, one hand on a coalscuttle the other prickling across
    the butchered remains of my hair,
'What have you been reading, then?' I ask her,
experimenting, experimenting.
                      (Fisher, 2005: 261–2)

Slightly self-consciously, perhaps, Fisher establishes from the very beginning that both the texts and the relationship are, somehow, experimental. The time is at "dusk", where the crepuscular lends itself to the liminality of the moment, neither day nor night, in which the fingers are isolated and ironised within the metaphor "white like unlit electric bulbs". The fingers are at once confined and confining, unable to release light to lighten. Then Fisher uses a seemingly exophoric "this" in "This green goes with this purple." "This" is exophoric from the speech that contains it, that is, it refers outside and away from its immediate context in the discourse. As such, it might appear to refer out to the colour of the walls, or carpet, or ceiling, or even items of clothing. In referring out of its discourse context, it pulls the reader into the room but without specifying what it is that the reader is "looking at" or perceiving; thus the scene's indeterminacy is confirmed. The figurative interior contains colour but not the surface the colour stains.

In the next stanza, Fisher gives indications of the interior in a way which seems very class specific. The details of the armchair, fireplace, coal-scuttle, and the colours of the scene, not only the green and purple alluded to in the first stanza but also the dark brown of the armchair in the second, seem entirely typical of the dull, dark interiors of post-war Britain. It is noticeable, then, that Fisher repeats the lines "Squatting beside a [...] of my hair" in the final verse of the piece, creating an empirically realized context for the two people.

What also intensifies the liminality of the piece is the sense of the dialogue as full of non-sequiturs. Grice's model of conversation, the "Cooperative Principle" describes expectations created in the hearer by the speaker. These expectations were based on four maxims: Quality, that the speaker be telling the truth; Quantity, that the speaker gives neither too little or too much information: Relation, that the utterance be relevant to the hearer; and, Manner, that the utterance be clear enough for the speaker to understand it (Grice, 1989). It is clear from the speeches isolated above, and the free indirect speech that Fisher interpolates at points in the piece, that there is considerable flouting of all four of Grice's Maxims. When in the woman's first turn, the woman asks the persona/narrator about the colours the relevance of the narrator's reply, "Old sexy-eyes" seems minimal, unless by some quirk of fate the woman has one green and one purple eye. The maxim of

the fisher syndrome explained

Manner is flouted because the utterance is quite unclear to the reader and by the narrator's own admission, "is all I say"; so flouts the Maxim of Quantity. Of course, whether or not the utterance flouts the Maxim of Quality depends upon the speaker and hearer's own understanding and not the reader's. Thus, the reader is held between his or her own reading and the relationship which is offered as part of the 'meaning' of the text. The relationship between the man and the woman is liminal in that they seem to understand the various presuppositions that their flouting of the Maxim of Quantity creates, and it is the reader outside the relationship who is confused.

The reader might assume that the next conversational turn "I've tried tonight. This place!" belongs to the narrator, and the woman's next turn "Doesn't *welcome* me" might support that; whereby, the relevance of "I've tried tonight", with the ellipsis of the object after the verb tried, i.e., "tried *what* tonight", might be explained by the narrator's having tried to clean his room up, to decorate it. However, of course, that assumption, in Grice's terms the "implicature", would be undermined by reference back to the woman's comment about the matching of the green with the purple, as if she were responsible for the decoration, etc. of the room.

At the end of this piece, the narrator and the woman move into a chant about the moon. This violation of the Maxim of relation has rather less to do with conversation, and more to do with its position in a text that purports to be a poem. The relation of the utterances about the moon is secured by the use of the pro-form "it", the use of "we" to link the narrator and the woman in mutual perception of the moon, and linking of the phrasal subject "And when the moon with horror" to its verbal predicate "comes blundering blind up the side" by the narrator. The central relevance of the phrases to each other, for the reader, I would suggest, is in the continuation of the rhythmic impulse between the two speakers. It is perhaps, the Maxim of Manner that appears violated to the reader because of the description of the "action of the Moon". The two speakers appear to share a mutual understanding, which the reader can witness but not satisfactorily elucidate.

Finally, the narrator utters the only "transactional" utterance of the whole conversation, "What have you been reading, then?", whose literalness of meaning offers a final moment of humour, and release.

What may be useful about this kind of analysis is that it offers us a way into the surrealism of Fisher's writing at that time, and its implications for later developments in the relationship of Fisher's writing about the other. In 'Experimenting' from 1962, Fisher consciously violates the linearity of conversation; whether this is out of some internal dynamic in his writing, or out of Fisher's acknowledged debt to surrealism. The 'I' of this poem negotiates a meaning with the woman that excludes the reader. In this sense, the other is held at a point of understanding that is not realised, even though the context of the nineteen fifties room is not only made explicit but emphasized by repetition. As Royle comments, "[the uncanny] is not 'out there', in any simple sense: as a crisis of the proper and natural, it disturbs any straightforward sense of what is inside and what is outside". The reader of this piece is held on the inside of the room observing its detail thanks to the effortless precision that Fisher creates not through realisation of empirical detail but by suggestion and the interplay of non-sequiturs from the human inhabitants of the scene. That pulling of the reader into the scene only further serves to disturb that "straightforward sense of what is inside and what is outside" as the reader is trapped in the effort of making that "sense".

RICHARD PRICE

'Ear-jewels catch a glint': *The Half-Year Letters*

The Half-Year Letters is an alphabet book designed and realised by the artist Ronald King using specially commissioned text by Roy Fisher. It was published in 1983. Each letter of the alphabet is made manifest as a pop-up which is not actually printed but ingeniously cut and folded from the paper of the page itself. Fisher's free verse appears under each letter. It is one of several collaborations King and Fisher have made over more than three decades of association, though these have usually been larger and more overtly complex works such as *Bluebeard's Castle* (1972–3), *The Left-Handed Punch* (1986), and *Tabernacle* (1986).

Two short accounts of *The Half-Year Letters* by Cathy Courtney and Matthew Sperling give, respectively, musical and literary approaches to the book. Cathy Courtney describes the genesis of the book as a development of an earlier project with King, *Scenes from an Alphabet* (Circle Press, 1978). *Scenes* features pop-ups of A, B, and C only, with an acrostic poem by Fisher, the alphabet itself forming the first letter of each of the twenty-six lines. It was Fisher's encouragement that saw King extend the pop-ups in later years to the whole alphabet: 'Roy Fisher was integral to the idea, urging King to invent the full twenty-six letters.' (Courtney, 140).

Courtney suggests that Fisher's experience as a jazz pianist is one way to approach an understanding of *The Half-Year Letters* and corroborates this with Fisher's reflection on his role:

> My accompaniment on 'The Half-Year Letters' was of a musical nature. Ron already had a very dogmatic master text, so I thought I would have a voice and a disposition muttering along with his letters. (Courtney, 140)

Fisher's wry use of "dogmatic" here affectionately imagines the alphabet and perhaps even King as strict taskmasters. It seems to me this way of seeing King's art is critical to how Fisher's texts, by contrast, behave. King's letters are capital letters, an aspect of their authority that Fisher is playing off and 'against'. Another authoritative aspect is the alphabet's 'given' nature—given in the sense that King has sent them to Fisher to work on but also because the sequence of the alphabet is canonical. Dogmatics tend to think their sequence of events is pre-ordained, in 'the nature of things', and are perhaps most dogmatic when their view's central assertions are in fact the most chancy. The alphabet has become so familiar that it seems unquestionable in that way, Fisher suggests, an irrefutable organic object instead of the artificial object it actually is. (Or perhaps the alphabet is neither one nor the other, is, like a very old building, somewhere between nature and artifice?) In any case Fisher here signals a re-perspectivising of it (again, I stress that this is a humorous use of the word "dogmatic").

In the nature of pop-ups, the letters jut out into the reading space of the page creating sculpture in a traditional place of contemplation—the book, not the temple or the gallery. However, far from the children's book genre in which pop-ups usually reside, King's are made only of cuts and folds in the paper and do not form an extravagant and brightly coloured structure (in children's books an elaborate boat, say, a tree, or an animal). In this sense King is himself playing off and against a 'given' but in the exact opposite direction from Fisher's. Fisher's texts, on the contrary, are busy—perhaps as busy as the pop-ups a reader might expect in such a book. As Matthew Sperling writes, "Fisher's text imagines language as a material medium so alive with conflictual energies that it can rise off the page, and exist in three-dimensions, like a pop-up image." (Sperling, 1451). Fisher's poems describe a number of different (adult) activities which are nevertheless not dwelt on in detail; their texts are often rushing so quickly they are syntactically incomplete. No verse is full-stopped at the end of the page, giving the jump from section to section sometimes a minimalist suspension (when the text has, despite my overview, a haiku-like staticity) but more often a kind of lurch.

These texts have been called prose poetry, or rather a "species of 'poet's prose'" (Sperling, 1451), an observation which strengthens a link of affinity made earlier by Marjorie Perloff when she suggested that Fisher and the North American L=A=N=G=U=A=G=E poets shared a surprisingly close approach to avant-garde prose, Fisher anticipating the poets across the Atlantic in his *The Cut Pages* (Fulcrum, 1971), 'Roy Fisher's "Language Book"' (Perloff, unnumbered). That may be, but I think the genre categorisation for *The Half-Year Letters* is incorrect: the

the fisher syndrome explained

---

lineation of the texts is almost always of poetry not prose, sometimes enjambed, sometimes endstopped, but always verse. Even the possible exception, the text for 'N' (which I will discuss a little later), though it is among the most prose-like, has such suspenseful prepositions in key line-endings it could still be defended as free verse. The others are much more clearly poetry. Here is 'H' for example, with the fertility of its searching line-end pauses:

> There's a belief to fix. It feels strong,
> it feels far off.
> There is no faith to defile by fragmentation,
> to fit into half faiths or less

This isn't necessarily a pedantic point: I think that Fisher's free verse, often linked to jazz aesthetics, leads to various effects on the meaning of the sequence, including its aural nature, to which I'll also return.

First, however, back to the visuality of *The Half-Year Letters*, and especially to the striking difference between King's approach and Fisher's. The contrast between the two artists' contributions is so stark that King may have felt that each actually needed a little protection from each other: when Courtney interviewed King about the design of the book she asked him about the blue line that runs between pop-up and text: "Well that was really to separate off the poem from the letter" (King, 501). It's a blue line, not a black one, and I read it as gentler and more porous because of that, but a line it is (perhaps it could even be the 'thin blue line' of a police force separating, the Line might like to think, the alphabet's elite from Fisher's rabble, but that may be to carry things too far). Another effect is that the line evokes at the exposed outside edges of the book, in a modern, asymmetrical, way, binder's thread, a material actually absent from this elastic, bellows-like structure. When the illusion is discovered it serves to emphasise the non-conventional aspect of the accordion binding.

King doesn't mention another effect the line has, which is to complement, rather than contrast with, the bustling ever-onwards nature of Fisher's text: internally the line visually moves the book across each page and then onwards from page to page. Fisher's choice of making the work a calendar or diary—each opening corresponds to a week (there being fifty-two weeks in a full year, hence the 'half-year letters' of the twenty-six letter alphabet)—means that King's blue line is a *time*-line, contributing to the book's propulsive call to turn from the one page into the next, and so into next week. It is likely that King added the line later and so was in turn responding to Fisher's text, the genuine to-ing and fro-ing of collaborators in art. King is celebrated for, among other aspects of his work, his use of exuberant collaging and warm colour (which has been variously associated with his Brazilian upbringing, his interest in African masks, and, later, his London studio's location on the route of the Notting Hill carnival). However, these pop-ups display a quite different but enduring element that has perhaps been under-acknowledged: austerity, abstraction; depth in the minimal. This is something that Fisher, in interview, does identify in King's solo works but, perhaps because of the highly complex larger scale works he was also involved in with King, doesn't associate with their collaborations:

> I don't see myself as restraining Ron, explicitly or tacitly. I think rather, that by inviting me to be his collaborator he implicitly asks me to hold his coat, that is to say to embody for a while the classical or austere part of himself while he indulges in freedoms he might otherwise feel inclined to rein in. In his non-collaborative works the purity is often clearly central. You could reverse the proposition and say that in our collaborations I can indulge my passion for parsimonious writing to the full, safe in the knowledge that sustained invention and feats of technical virtuosity can be counted on to be provided by the artist. (Lambirth, 141–4)

Fisher is of course right, though, about King's extraordinary technical accomplishment as anyone who contemplates the elegance and concealed complexity of the folded cut-out pop-ups will realise. The result is a breathtaking purity but one that is soft-edged, delicate: that there is no actual printer's ink used for the cut-outs means that the letters rely on subtle contrast and shadow for their definition. Fisher's verses allude to the joint project as a sculptural one, the initiating letter A suggesting that the book at this stage is the block of stone that begins

the fisher syndrome explained

---

a sculpture or other work of construction—"Half-year starts out of the quarry"—but the sculpture is as light as a feather. Further along in the sequence the fragmentary sentence in the letter M, "In a book of marked megaliths", captures the sculptural (and mysterious) nature of King's lettering. Perhaps even this however does not quite touch the paradox of the letters' forceful yet delicate imposition. Instead Fisher arguably finds an analogue across the whole of his text in the many references to part-states, half-ness, compromises in clarity (smoke, veils, and glints that actually emphasise the murk of their surroundings); like the letters these descriptions seem to rely on the emergence but weightlessness of light for their discernment.

There is also the aural to think about. Fisher's reference to himself "muttering along" to the letters confers a kind of sound quality not just to his own poetry but to King's shapes: it's as if the pop-ups aren't just visual but are powerful one-letter utterances, thought-clarifying not just as physical works of art but as the one-syllable words of meditative practice. Fisher's "muttering" also implies the eyes-to-heaven attitudes of the bright resentful servant (think of Mutley and Dick Dastardly if you like), though of course Fisher's is a mock-resentment here, and it foregrounds distorted speech as a response to the breathtaking clarity of King's letters. Such creative accompaniment only confirms, as Courtney rightly suggests, that Fisher is here as much the jazz player elaborating around a rocksteady bass as he is the poet (Courtney, 140).

Yet the story is more complex on both sides of the partnership. In a note by Fisher on the last page of the book a further structuring device is revealed. The reader now finds out that it was not just that the text had to relate to the alphabet, but that there was a controlled vocabulary to be peppered throughout the work. Moreover, as the reader might now expect, even the relationship to the alphabet was never intended to be straightforward. Fisher now confirms what will have gradually dawned on the reader: that acrostics were always going to be out because he had set the rules in such a way that the letter in question could be within the body of a word rather than, as in more traditional alphabet books, always at the beginning.

Richard Price

THE TEXT treats the rigorous forward movement of an alphabet as a movement
    through time, as if it marked the twenty-six weeks of a half-year, April through
    September. The vocabulary for each letter, a week, is governed in part by the
    pervading presence of the letter, in a variety of uses; in part by a chance operation
    based on a set of key words—half, year, quarry, bread, candle, swan, blunder,
    job, booze, burnt, trick, door, rider, wild, glisten, veil, lope, vigil, smoke, vex,
    prize, open, swift, fit, fix—each of which is particularly likely to occur in the
    company of one of the letters which spell it.

The restricted set of terms contains several words of the kind I've already mentioned: they are to do with reduced light, or points of illumination within an environment of otherwise subdued light—candle, glisten, veil, smoke. In the book at large Fisher adds to the atmospherics of these using cognate words that are not on his self-imposed list (such a list is also a kind of 'dogma' by the way—clearly Fisher relishes such parameters to work with): pall, twilight, dull, dusk, and glint. Other words from the locked-down kist of special words suggest movement implicitly or explicitly—blunder, rider, wild, lope, open, and swift.

There are several mysteries associated with this list. Is there something drily amusing in having such a large 'restricted' list for such a minimal text? Surely there is something odd about having 25 words, just one short of the number of letters in the actual alphabet, rather than the full 26. A further curiosity is the under-played use Fisher makes of this vocabulary. Several of his words could double as two different forms of grammar (especially, both verb and noun), a quality that poets would normally exploit for switches of meaning in the sort of permutational form that *Half-Year Letters* is. Perhaps this is Fisher again avoiding another kind of expectation, or demonstrative simply of the fact that the verb-noun 'flick' is not part of Fisher's poetry scape, not part of his sensibility: in this way in *The Half-Year Letters* "swift" is

the fisher syndrome explained

---

fast but never the flitting creature; "smoke" is never an active verb but rather drifts in and out of the sequence solely in noun-y clouds. Perhaps the conclusion to be made here is that although there is clearly play and humour in the text, some of which is based on the re-use of vocabulary in surprising contexts, such play seems relatively low down in the mix, an obliquity without the demonstrative tease of such grammatical pivots.

So far this vocabulary gives a greyish, glimmering palette to Fisher's poetry, but what, some pre-readers may ask, is the sequence actually about?

For some this will be a crass question: because the text could be said to be so abstracted as to be, as it were, musical, so making the reception of tone all (in which case that glimmer-in-the-grey and its metaphoric diffusions *is* what the text is about); because to talk of pressing quickly on to 'a' 'subject' is to give in to a satisfaction-on-demand culture characterised by the bold philistine certainties of both retail and the media (certainties which nevertheless seem invested with caprice); and because the pedagogy of poetry should emphasise formal qualities above informational substance ("Mere subject matter? Go to the novel and the film for that…").

My own view is that a praising of the paratactic should not obliterate the freight and minute interaction of detail that these texts carry, especially as to do so may encourage an ideological interpretation on a category-praised but essentially unscrutinised text (old fashioned parataxis as the continuous revolution in literature).

What is *The Half-Year Letters* about? In a sense, the title is the label. Nouns first: 'Letters'. We've already seen indications of how self-conscious the text is about the book itself—as well as the sculptural examples above, think of the letter M's sentence "By empty morning roads to a hump-backed / bridge." As if it contained a shadow of an Anglo-Saxon riddle, this seems to me to be a quiet reference to M as the last letter before the doubled book needs to be turned over for the remaining half of the alphabet: 'M', sharing an intervening silence with 'N'—that silence is the true halfway of the even-numbered alphabet—is the beginning of the book's bridge. Is there even an allusion to the letter M, King's cut-out, as looking like a bridge? It certainly does. The reader might also note Fisher's enjambment of "hump-backed /

bridge"—that's an apt jolt for such a crossing and again reminds the reader that free verse rather than prose poetry is the active genre here. In the letter H, Fisher again seems to be talking about the book when he says "Half reconciled, half healed: but two / different sets of halves that won't match". (Of course he is talking much more generally as well, with a melancholy sense of unease.) Again look at the function of the enjambment as it pressures the word "different" at the beginning of that last line. All this suggests that one of the topics of this book, is the nature of the book …

Adjectives second: *Half-Year*. Time's registration is a theme in the book, as the calendar element demonstrates. There are diary-like entries—"A queasy request in the mail" ('Q'), "Then in hard-blown sun to the uplands / above the used-up quarries and burnt houses" ('U'). This betrays one of the origins of the text—Fisher "took a random starting date from his own diaries and extracted events and observations from a twenty-six week span. From these he selected a group of words associated with the notes […]" (Courtney, 140). That said, many of the poems in the sequence are less direct than this, or suggest not a single event but, montage-like, a continuousness of activity across a more extended period of time: "Open season for old wounds, odd jobs; / loping from door to door, hovering, / hamming it up, on the booze" ('O'); "A burnt year. Trick riders blunder about / the concrete, without quarry or prize" (from 'R'); "Burnt sugar; / and blunder to London, lie frog-flat under / a black pall, wake in the after-smoke, / a huge bee at the window" (for 'B' … playfully). In one poem, 'G', Fisher's text seems to be reaching towards a sensual understanding of time, a palpability and freshness that tries to elude the strict measurement that time of course is: "Vigil glistens through into the night, / under a veil of vagueness. Still left in it / there's a virginity that won't tell the time."

'Vigil', one of the recurring words from the given set of vocabulary, is a temporal word that offers, as it were, slow time, the state of concerned waiting: initial impressions of hyperactivity in Fisher's sequence really do need to be modified to convey a greater sense of the different time signatures occurring across the work, rather than relentless full speed ahead. In the same way there is nothing hyperactive in the letter N:

the fisher syndrome explained

> The spirals of the snail shells I found in the
> dawn, scattered in the carbonized stubble
> of the charred canal bank at Swanbank:
> some shells burnt white, others still
> patterned, a glisten of mucus left at
> their openings

There is after all something awkward, interim, and certainly unliterary about a half-year diary, normally a form of business stationery. I think the sequence's internal moving from images of bluster and the frantic to solitary reflection and back again reflect at micro level the abbreviated diary's insecurity of balance, a restlessness which encompasses a spectrum between the frenetic and the static, the exhausted, even.

There is much more in the text, however, than is signalled by the title. The visually reduced palette of whites, blacks, greys and glimmer certainly resonates with the post-industrial landscape that this and other poems by Fisher describe even as the focus veers between the close-up-and-personal (the glint of ear-rings, a ringed hand on a page) to broader scapes (a quarry-side vista). To me the text, as with the artist's book as a whole, becomes in itself a metaphor for the reduced knowledge that one can only ever have of anyone else, with the compressed entries for each letter offering not only a tone of intrigue, evidencing such unknowability, but, as with a particular perhaps Beckettian strand of minimalism, suggesting with more than a pang vast emotional depths. As such the text proceeds as much as a series of dreams as a series of recorded facts. The scorched snails by the canal-side in 'N' are intensely if imagistically 'real' but there is the mystery of what precisely the voice was doing there as a witness. On second look there is also that lyrical aestheticisation of the shells in the observation of their heat-wiped pallor and the remains of 'pattern' (I think of the blank pop-outs again and the pattern of words beneath them, and the suggestion that time can be experienced not only as a measure but as heightened feeling, perhaps called art). A third look and there is the curious placing of that text between two other quite different verses, 'M' and 'O', all of whose connection only seems to make sense as a function of the voice's (and book's) wayward momentum, the nearly discontinuous in the human now marshalled and propelled by the book.

There is of course much more to say about *The Half-Year Letters*, and much more than can be said here. The odd temperature variations in tone, it seems to me, need more scrutiny. Take for instance the spiky contempt the text reserves for academic careerists ("A thesis to turn a trick comes swiftly to / trial. The fate that fits it is to be burnt" (from 'T'). Elsewhere there are troubled ("vexed") responses to faith and belief; there is the recurrence of a Rider figure, "The Rider Interrupted by Anniversaries" as the voice in the letter 'I' puts it; and there are instances of hearing impairment—sometimes deafness figured as hapless gaucherie ("Blundering in deaf through the door"). All these and more contribute to a text which manages to be leaf-light and "rich" at the same time, a feat entirely in keeping with Ron King's realised design, making it a book to return to again and again.

References

The collaborations made by Ron King and Roy Fisher over the decades can be seen in the collections of the British Library. I am grateful to the Library for allowing me time to work on this article, and to the poet Peter McCarey for his comments on an earlier draft.

Courtney, Cathy, *The Looking Book: a pocket history of Circle Press, 1967–96*, 1996.
Fisher, Roy and Ronald King, *The Half-Year Letters: an alphabet book*, Guildford: Circle Press, 1983. British Library shelfmark: Cup.510.bha.7.
King, Ronald, with Cathy Courtney, *Ron King interviewed by Cathy Courtney*, London: British Library, 1996. Transcript of recording C466/47/01 F5422A.
Lambirth, Andrew, with descriptions and commentary by Ron King, *Cooking the Books: Ron King and the Circle Press*, New Haven: Yale Center for British Art, 2002.
Perloff, Marjorie, 'Roy Fisher's "Language Book"', Electronic Poetry Center,http://wings.buffalo.edu/epc/authors/perloff/articles/fisher.html, Unnumbered, undated; accessed 21/8/09.
Sperling, Matthew, '"The Making of the Book": Roy Fisher, the Circle Press and the Poetics of Book Art', in *Literature Compass* 4/5 (2007), pp.1444–1459.

PETER ROBINSON
Collected and Recollected

Liberties in Context

When does a tension become a contradiction? Or when does a contradiction cease to generate vital quandaries and instead negate itself? Can such negations authenticate and set free? Or do they cancel out? These questions are prompted by the new, somewhat chronological reordering of Roy Fisher's writings in *Poems 1955–1980*, which brings back into print most (though not all, as advertised) of Fisher's published poetry and prose between those dates. A tension is referred to in the book's 'blurb': "Roy Fisher's work is a unique mixture in British post-war poetry of English 'provincialism' of subject-matter with internationalism of style and aesthetics." It is characterized, as John Ash writes in the *Atlantic Review*, by a tension between "the traditions of English empiricism on the one hand and the perceptual experimentation and formal artifice of European modernism on the other." There is indeed a tension between Fisher's English "provincialism" and international modernism; but, just as the former -ism must be dressed up between inverted commas, so its tensed opposite might be dressed down as "international". This is not because the sources for Fisher's methods are actually confined to England, far from it; these sources do, nonetheless, retain a recherché, distant glamour. An early poem, 'Leaving July', collected for the first time, describes how

> Low crippled clouds drag on a naked sky
> over night leaves that point
> ravines of darkest green down steeply
> from the pale plateau of glaucous twilight;
>
> the sky flattens on the land and gazes
> back up into itself with rainwater eyes
> out of blue rutted sockets on a builder's site.

The word glaucous, "of dull greyish green or blue", shows the stamp of its country of origin through the botanical meaning "covered with bloom as of grapes", the produce of Mediterranean Latin and Greek.

Peter Robinson

A recent usage associates it with France and modernism in England by means of the title to 'Yeux Glauques' in Pound's *Hugh Selwyn Mauberley*. Travelling by the lines "Thin like brook-water, / With a vacant gaze", Fisher drops it off in the English provinces where "rainwater eyes" gaze "out of blue rutted sockets on a builder's site".

Tensing the local and the European allowed Fisher, at first, to present a context—the local—without being obliged to use the language familiarly associated with or attached to it. 'Toyland', another early piece, and a poem that could be cited to endorse Fisher's English "provincialism" of subject-matter, shows him chafing against the obligation to stick with the words that are predicated by the context, words received that fit and seem fitting: "I might by exception see an ambulance or the fire brigade / Or even, if the chance came round, street musicians (singing and playing)." Here the brackets are a cough around stating the obvious: the point where the "formality", about which the poem divagates, becomes just a formality. Inversely, this tension is a scheme for importing words that will retain their foreign local colour, as in "glaucous" above, without bringing with them their locality or context. Fisher's Europe is that of the stay-at-home pressing his nose to a travel-agent window; his different modernisms, various forms of impure diction.

The obligations of context—where a word is located—may bespeak further senses of relation. For if it is the potential to become "just a formality" that puts the copula at risk, composing informally within a context can release some of the density of the habitual and familiar, a density thinned by constant recognition. But the refusal of predication or the avoidance of syntactic obligations, rather than necessarily thwarting mere habituation, may render the work down into only inert bits, frustrated pieces. The poem 'At No Distance' hovers precariously on this precipice. In the earlier collage of prose and poetry, *City*, Fisher uses relative clauses to indicate the distances in a family that are disclosed through war. His poem 'The Entertainment of War', disparaged for its unchallenging familiarity by the poet himself in *19 Poems and an Interview* (1975), is nonetheless an early essay in Russian Formalism's *priem ostrannenija*, "the device of making it strange", which was discussed by Donald Davie in *Thomas Hardy and British Poetry* with regard to more overtly defamiliarizing works such as 'As He Came Near

the fisher syndrome explained

Death' and 'Three Ceremonial Poems'. In 'The Entertainment of War', the strangeness is integral to the events, so that despite the conventional narrative mode, the habitual life of the family is distorted, giving fresh density to habit, through the bombing:

> When I saw it, the house was blown clean by blast and care:
> Relations had already torn out the new fireplaces;
> My cousin's pencils lasted me several years.

Vacuuming is imaginatively enmeshed with sudden, quick death in the ambivalences of "blown clean", occasioning the "blast" unexpectedly and aptly followed by "care". The relations have picked the corpse of the house to the bone, and the poet as a boy is closely involved in the sharing out of distant relatives' property:

> These were marginal people I had met only rarely
> And the end of the whole household meant that no grief was
>   seen;
> Never have people seemed so absent from their own deaths.

The concluding prose paragraphs of *City*, in the 1968 revised version, combine a familiarity which is not contemptuous, because properly distant, and a separateness that is not just one thing after another, because syntactically related:

> I have often felt myself to be vicious, in living so much by the eye, yet among so many people. I can be afraid that the egg of light through which I see these bodies may present itself as a keyhole. Yet I can find no sadism in the way I see them now. They are warm-fleshed, yet their shapes have the miniscule, remote morality of some mediaeval woodcut of the Expulsion: an eternally startled Adam, a permanently bemused Eve. I see them as homunculi, moving privately each in a softly lit fruit in a nocturnal tree. I can consider without scorn or envy the wellfound bedrooms I pass, walnut and rose-pink, altars of tidy, dark-haired women, bare-necked, wifely. Even in these I can see order.

The paragraph has to skirt being touching, in a weak sense, so as to remotely touch on the private lives of "so many people" in a city. Not only does it see order, but constructs it generously. The "well-found" bedrooms are built on sound foundations, and in the separate, yet interrelated, points of attention through which the syntax moves the poet not only finds them successfully, he finds them in good health.

The releases and unexpectedness that occur in Fisher's writing on human and domestic relations have a necessary obliquity and a distance that could free the poet in *City* from what he has called, in discussing the somewhat later poem 'For Realism': "the entailments of [things] in ordinary reality", while still describing: "a place which was real to me, a place with family association". This release from context, from what might be called the over-determination of a familial landscape, may have been a necessity for Fisher—and the contrary need to remain in context is also evidenced above. Yet the aesthetic allegiances Fisher took on proved, with *City* in the first place, peculiarly suited to what was occurring in that landscape. "On one of the steep slopes that rise towards the centre of the city all of the buildings have been destroyed within the past year", *City* begins, and later:

> The new city is bred out of a hard will, but as it appears, it shows itself a little ingratiating, a place of arcades, passages, easy ascent, good light. The eyes twinkle, beseech and veil themselves; the full, hard mouth, the broad jaw—these are no longer made visible to all.

By the time international modernism in architecture reached the English provincial cities it was already approximately half a century old. When Fisher, in *City*, creates a tension between a prose style to describe, among other things, the minutiae of the older Victorian city and a poetry of half-anxious refrains, he effects an overall heterogeneity of styles in the work which represents a sponsoring tension in the city itself. So, for example, his modernism in 'Lullaby and Exhortation for the Unwilling Hero' includes an allusion to one thirty-year-old archetype for the style, T.S. Eliot's *The Waste Land*. "What are the roots that clutch, what branches grow / Out of this stony rubbish?" is scaled down and secularly reformulated as "What steps descend, what rails

the fisher syndrome explained

conduct?"—the borrowed lines of a provincial city's shopping precinct. But the prose quoted above holds the figure in a densely equivocal stance that embraces nostalgia for the Victorian "full, hard mouth", an architecture that dwarfed the city's inhabitants, and an equally qualified enchantment with the glassy modern style—a semi-transparent illusion, half concealing a hard will. And the quiet, almost disinterested tone of *City* keeps these ambivalences tensed. A decade or so later that tense poise has become a blunted sarcasm at the discrepancy between the international modernist provincial architecture and a "social realism", the latter term in this case synonymous with social disillusion as here in 'Artists, Providers, Places to Go':

> The little figures in the architect's drawing
> the sleep of reason begets
> little figures.
>
> Nose the car up through the ramps
> into a bay, and leave it,
> keys in the dash by regulation—
> cost-effective:
> come back and find it gone,
> you got free parking.

'Seven Attempted Moves', from some five years earlier, with its concluding "Confinement, / shortness of breath. / Only a state of mind. / And / Statues of it built everywhere", can still gasp sceptically, without sounding so down in the mouth.

The precariousness of Fisher's vital discontinuities founded on the potentially contradictory need for a freed, freeing diction and the obligations of contextual or local necessity can be felt in two transitional poems, 'Suppose—' and 'Continuity': the latter being the first poem Fisher wrote after a two-year silence from approximately 1968 to 1970. 'Suppose—', which begins: "Suppose that once in a while / It still works, just as it used to", goes on to doubt the strength of "realistic" notation by following "Curtained from street flashes / By afternoon clatter, / A crowd of faces and feet", with the shrugging gesture: "That sort of thing"; and equally doubts the value of Fisher's "1905 Modernist" sources, before summoning up the confidence to conclude:

> Why Alexandr Blok, the beautiful,
> Dealt out humbug,
> Still made sense —

'Continuity' acknowledges itself islanded in the familiar without urgency: 'Purpose? No purpose. Apparitions? None'. Yet in essaying a mild description it effects an un-emphatic analogy for the difficulty the poet has in swimming beyond the forms he has made in time:

> The fish-trap gives the water form,
> Minimal form, drawn on the current unattended,
> The lure and the check. So much free water.

A poetic agnosticism sensible in 'Minimal form', or the lines "The old flat arrangement, / Dry track of half a voice" and "Just enough light to ask questions by" from 'Suppose—', has employed the "realism" that is "only common sense" to doubt aesthetic freedoms and set the freedom from a habituated contextual necessity, which aesthetic sophistication may confer, to run down localized notation. These two poems succeed by living dangerously near the edge where tensed contraries cancel each other out.

Roy Fisher's work in the 1970s shows the tensed contraries in gestures of conflict which only occasionally result in the vital quandaries noted above. '107 Poems' and 'In The Wall' could be cited as among such exceptions. 'The Only Image' begins with a tiny observation ("Salts work their way / to the outside of a plant pot and dry white") and concludes:

>   I can
> compare what I like to the salts,
> to the pot, if there's a pot,
> to the winter if there's a winter.
>
> The salts I can compare
> to anything there is.
> Anything.

the fisher syndrome explained

John Ash notes that "it is a wry comment on the absolute arbitrariness and willfulness of imagination. It records a realist's defeat". Such an apt account has two crucial weaknesses, however, weaknesses inherent in the poem. First, "the absolute arbitrariness and wilfulness of imagination" is a formula that does not distinguish between the many forms of mental activity that relate things, ranging perhaps from pure delusion to clear intuition. The imaginative freedom to relate the disparate in an unstable, variable or effaced context is what the poem evidently asserts, but in doing so it has as little to say as John Ash about what exactly is to be compared to what and why; that is, nothing about how one connectedness, or one abutted disconnectedness, may be preferred to another; nothing about just, necessary relations. If it is the imagination which discloses such relations, and syntax—in however attenuated a form—which bears them, then it is merely the illusion of choice that is substituted for a functional relation when the imaginable is multiplied to infinity. Secondly, if 'The Only Image' records "a realist's defeat", it is a pyrrhic victory for the imagination. "Realism" inflicts terrible losses on imagination in "The salts I can compare / to anything there is". For "anything there is" places the poem's consciousness back in this strictly limited context: a rigid world of atomistically perceived things. Here an implicit contradiction cancels itself to nothing.

A similar cancelling occurs in 'Handsworth Liberties'. *Poems 1955–1980* includes a condensed, revised version of Fisher's note on *The Thing About Joe Sullivan* (1978) for the Poetry Book Society Bulletin. It indicates that this cancelling out is pressed on the writer by an inner necessity, from which the sequence arises, but which is effaced in the composition. The note describes how 'a gratuitous visual impression, always of some actual but quite inconsequential location—a street corner or suburban-industrial vista—near my home' would attach itself to a particular piece of music and be recalled each time the music was heard. "At length I decided that these visual memories had persisted for so long in laying claim to my attention that I would round on them and put them to work ... Writing the poems did not banish the images, but they came to seem less intrusive." In the earlier version of this note the last sentence read: "I still experience the images, but they have been subjected to a genial exorcism." Exorcising the intrusive, these poems are a relief from phantasmagoria (a Poundian term describing the visual imaginations of poets for whom "whole countrysides, stretches of hill and forest travel with them"). The eighth poem finds relief by projecting a residual context in which the art of "making strange" is extended to include perception without memory:

> At the end of the familiar,
> throwing away the end
> of the first energy, regardless;
> nothing for getting home with—

The poem acknowledges what is restricting about this peculiar receptivity to things without recognition or recall: the effacement of those social habituations that make a return home possible. But the contradictions proliferate here too, for if "nothing has a history", as the poem notes, there can be no such place as "home". Concluding, the poem gestures at its lost connections: "Getting home—getting home somehow, / late, late and small." Fended off by that "somehow" is the contextual density of the "late and small" child's-eye-view of a familial landscape compounded of the strange and those family ties that facilitate return. But the poem is not a child's-eye-view. Its aesthetic formulations are those of a poet with a history of his own styles in mind. The programmatic tone of the writing seeks to reconstruct by abstract statement the supposed disconnectedness of the wandering child's landscape, without the tonal burden of the situation that is alluded to in "late and small".

The abstracted calm in 'Handsworth Liberties' may exorcise the intrusive imagery, but it does not produce that sense of intrusiveness for the reader. The gripping, compelling quality of the imagery—as it is described in the note—has been replaced by pale annotations of context without obligation, without the necessary contingency of the familiar, but rather with occasional lists of familiar things: "a laundry— / brick, laurels, a cokeheap across from the cemetery gate— / a printing works and a small cycle factory; hard tennis courts". Fisher's note on the poems explains their lack of intrusion as a preferred state of affairs. While the sceptic in Fisher can find that the tension between the provincial and the international modernist serves as a way of doubting both, or can find his poems crippled by such doubts ('In The Black

the fisher syndrome explained

Country' makes self-mockery from the tentativeness of 'Suppose—'), the aesthetician can use the contradicting possibilities of his old tension to rule out what he no longer wants to have to be burdened with in poems. The discontinuities that created a spacious ground for tensed quandaries may serve him as a way out of his poems' inner necessity, leaving the reader with a neutral gesture—"late and small".

'Style', dedicated to Michael Hamburger, is a programme note to this aesthetic. It refuses the sense that style effects "intricacies of self and sign" or "the language of one's time / and class. The languages / of my times and classes" and prefers to

>   reach the air
> as a version by my friend Michael.
> He knows good Englishes.
> And he knows the language
> language gets my poems out of.

The poem prefers what may well have already been preferred. 'The Least', a poem from the early seventies, seems to have been inspired by Paul Celan's 'Ein Auge, Offen', and Hamburger's versions of Celan's 'Heimkehr' and 'Unten' may have contributed to the orientation of poem eight in 'Handsworth Liberties':

> Led home into oblivion
> the sociable talk of
> our slow eyes
>
> Led home, syllable after syllable …

In his introduction to *Paul Celan: Poems*, Hamburger notes the German poet's recognition that he could not treat his extreme loss of context and of family, through war and annihilation, "directly, realistically", yet also: "Very few of his German readers, for instance, could possibly be expected to know that Mapesbury Road—the title of another late poem — is a street in North West London where Celan used to visit a surviving relative, his father's sister, who is addressed in the poem". The attenuated distance between context and aesthetic gesture in Celan's work bares a pressure of experience, in experience's near effacement, that goes to authenticate the gesture. Yet when Fisher prefers to weaken or distance context by writing "the language / language gets my poems out of", a neutral version of Celan's straitened utterance, thus using Hamburger's often exemplary translatorese as a way of "getting his poems out of" (which can also mean "avoiding") a language bearing and betraying familiar ties, the liberties he takes have not that authenticating urgency in Celan which derives one of its sources from negation and effacement. The contradictions of context and diction are employed to evade by a cancelling negation the quandaries that they had begun by releasing. In adopting the language of translation, inevitably an English somewhat remote from its own or the original language's context, Fisher imports words without the burdensome entailments of their localities. Such an absence of burden in words is the very condition of work against which Hamburger's and indeed all translations to different degrees must struggle: conditions that necessitate translators' introductions. Fisher's 'A note on the Handsworth Liberties' serves a similar function, alluding to a distant or hardly to be felt context from which the poems rise. It is a gesture of responsibility, as he might be implying in 'Wonders of Obligation' when he writes that the "things we make up out of language / turn into common property. / To feel responsible / I put my poor footprint back in"—or this would be one way to read them.

Keeping it Strange

A reader familiar with Roy Fisher's publishing history might imagine his contract for this new edition containing a rider that the book has to be distinctly different from his three earlier 'collected poems' volumes. Certainly Fisher has come up with a gathering of work that is his most complete to date (though by no means a Complete Poems) and one characteristically non-definitively open-ended. The words 'collected' or 'complete' are nowhere to be seen. The book's main title, *The Long and the Short of It*, alludes in one of its meanings to the literal fact that the volume contains all his longer works (his two Oxford collected volumes did not include 'The Cut Pages') as well as the vast majority of his shorter, short, and very short pieces. Fisher's work ranges from the five-line joke poem called 'Epic' to the short epic called 'A Furnace'. The

the fisher syndrome explained

---

book is by no means a complete Fisher, because it pointedly excludes a number of poems that have previously been collected ('Occasional Poem', on the death of John Berryman, or 'To the Supposed Dancer') and other possible candidates for inclusion that have been published in pamphlets or magazines ('Three Early Pieces', 'Abraham Darby's Bridge'). It also steers clear of any approach to the fairly large body of early, uncollected poems—such as the elegant 'The Lemon Bride'— cited and discussed by James Keery in his chapter from *The Thing about Roy Fisher: Critical Studies* (2000). The book collects for the first time a few early poems that had got away ('Kingsbury Mill'), the completed text of 'The Dow Low Drop', which had appeared in abbreviated form in the 1996 Bloodaxe *New and Selected Poems*, and quite a number of shorter, occasional, or elegiac poems written during the last decade or so.

The book is not as reliable as it might have been, containing an unhappy peppering of minor misprints and typos; and Fisher had long ago issued a statement on such textual slippage in 'Irreversible': "The *Atlantic Review* misspelled Kokoschka. / In three weeks he was dead." This book's "fine cracks", which by no means diminish the importance of its publication, are further sign that for the poet it is not one of those graveyards of performance described in 'Five Morning Poems from a Picture by Manet' as "splinters of fact stuck in the earth's fat rind." The poet notes in the Acknowledgements that "These poems no more amount to a biography than I do" and thus "an arrangement that seemed chronological" would be "false". This effectively damns the two Oxford volumes (1980 and 1988) to falsity, for some such rough arrangement—with the exception of 'The Ship's Orchestra', put at the back in an appendix—appeared to have been tried there. In *The Long and the Short of It* "nothing of the kind is attempted", and the resulting rearrangement of his works will provide an intriguingly coherent deployment of texts both for Fisher's long-time readers and those fortunate people who, coming upon his work for the first time, can encounter its uniqueness afresh. For the chronically chronologically minded, Fisher has added dates of composition after titles in the Index (though the mysterious dates '0000' after 'City' and 'Interiors with Various Figures' must—for the time being—stand as either collapses in the face of a too complex chronology, dada jokes, or merely production slip-ups). Fisher kindly acknowledges my "help in the preparation of this book"; for the record, my contribution involved no more than an acted-upon suggestion about what to do with the poems that didn't evidently fall into generic categories, plus a few pleas for inclusions, in some cases of which the poems' defence council was overruled by the presiding judge.

Even for those who know Fisher's work well, this book offers revealing and refreshing encounters and conjunctions. The texts have been ordered into nine sections, of which five could be described as 'generic'. The first contains long works such as 'City', 'The Ship's Orchestra', 'The Cut Pages', and 'A Furnace'. The third is made up of comedy poems like 'A Modern Story' about poetry competitions, 'Paraphrases' about the weird epistolary life of a poet with an international reputation and no books in print, or 'The Poetry Promise' about keeping the customer satisfied in these market-driven days, or 'The Nation'—written before the institution in the UK of a "National Poetry Day", but a perfectly judged mockery *avant la lettre* of such superficially populist, culturally retrograde antics. The fifth gathers poems dedicated to other writers and artists for *festschrifts*, memorials, or from no occasional prompting, such as 'Staffordshire Red' (for Geoffrey Hill), 'Emblem' (for Lorine Niedecker) and 'Songs from the Camel's Coffin' (for Gael Turnbull), its title borrowed from Turnbull's own 'For a Jazz Pianist', in which he describes "(a camel's coffin?)" as "a black / and polished upright / slotted box". The final section of Fisher's poem records his arrival in the USA for a visit that included a reading event at Notre Dame (where he was photographed playing one such camel's coffin, a photo subsequently printed in a university yearbook, captioned in the manner of 'Irreversible' as a picture of John Cage):

> Born in the middle of the island and never leaving it
> in fifty years, then startled
> on stepping down to the battered tarmac of O'Hare
> to discover that the air above it,
> the entire medium of elsewhere,
> wasn't as I'd guessed it would have to be, a heavy
> yellowish fluid tending towards glass,
> towards mica. Why in all that time

the fisher syndrome explained

had nobody said?
I'll never be sure, that's for certain.

Such lines as these casually instance Fisher's uniqueness—his ability to preserve a remarkable freshness in his encounters with the world, which we can then encounter too, refreshing our sense of the lived. This is not exactly a Russian formalist "making strange", because to Fisher the thing, in this case the air above O'Hare, is strange anyway. Fisher's art is about processing experience without lessening its strangeness. It is about *keeping* it strange—and this has required his never being "sure" and "that's for certain." Section VII of his book is devoted to the sequences and series of shorter writings, the 'Interiors with Various Figures', the 'Texts for a Film' about Birmingham that Tom Pickard produced, the 'Seven Attempted Moves', 'The Six Deliberate Acts', 'Five Morning Poems from a Picture by Manet', the four poems 'To the Memory of Wyndham Lewis', or the 'Three Ceremonial Poems'. Last of these generic groups, section VIII, is given over to collaborations with artists—such as 'Correspondence' with Tom Phillips, 'Also' with Derek Greaves, and the many others with Ronald King. Missing from this section though is 'Cultures', a collaboration with King (helpfully described by Ralph Pite in his chapter from *The Thing about Roy Fisher*) but one whose arrangement defies publication in a book of this kind.

While these five sections are the volume's reinforced structure, built upon the grounds of compositional habits and preferences, the other four sections—gatherings of poems that don't fit any of those generic categories—are, as far as the organization is concerned, the book's most revealing. These mid- or short-length poems tracking individual moments of inspiration contain borderline overlaps with other sections. 'The Thing about Joe Sullivan' might be thought Fisher's most dedicated poem, in that it expresses an overwhelming fascination with the psychology and aesthetics, and indeed ethics, of this white Chicagoan jazz pianist's style; but it doesn't appear in section V, presumably, because these two musicians—Fisher has also worked as a semi-professional jazz pianist—were not personally acquainted. Similarly, 'One World', a poem reporting on an early teaching experience with a remedial class at a school and reflecting on the unlikelihood that such pupils could have come to be readers of little magazines, might have appeared in the comedies section—since it was first published in one of the pamphlets of such work issued by the late Richard Caddel's Pig Press. Yet its account of teaching a class of severely underprivileged children is not, properly read, a joke at all. So the fascination of these more apparently ad-hoc sections lies in their prompting a reader to think about how and why specific works have found their way into each of these four and, further, why individual texts found there have become neighbours.

Section VI, for instance, appears to be made up of poems that variously address without satire Fisher's evolving awareness of his own aesthetics. Born in 1930, and not in 1885 or thereabouts, Fisher, though willing to give interviews, has felt no inclination to write manifestos, whether group or personal, or indeed to establish his 'poetics' by means of academic, critical, or hortatory prose—and especially not before the fact of having written attempts at pieces of literary art. Thus, 'For Realism', 'A Poem Not a Picture', 'The Lesson in Composition', 'Of the Empirical Self and for Me', or 'From an English Sensibility' come together with other relevant pieces to define, however obliquely and inconclusively, what Fisher has thought and felt he has been up to all these years. Nor does this section, since it is the occasional work of decades, pretend to offer a single, coherent aesthetic position. No sooner have we read the close of 'For Realism' ("A realism / tries to record, before they're gone, / what silver filth these drains have run"), than we encounter the six-line epigram 'It is Writing' which ends: "I mistrust the poem in its hour of success, / a thing capable of being / tempted by ethics into the wonderful." It is hard to believe that the latter, from 1974, has not been placed thus on the same page as a tacit comment on the former, written in 1965, and made a moral meal of by Donald Davie in the chapter 'Roy Fisher: An Appreciation' from *Thomas Hardy and British Poetry* (1973).

But why, then, asks the doubter, isn't 'The Thing about Joe Sullivan', with its tacit ethical-aesthetic commentary, or 'The Memorial Fountain' with its 'thirty-five-year-old-man, / poet, / by temper, realist, / watching a fountain'—why are these poems in section V, and not alongside 'For Realism' or the 'Lesson in Composition'? One pragmatic reason is that the various mid-length poems must not be lined up by overt or obvious similarities. If you put 'For Realism' next to 'The Memorial Fountain', for instance, you allow a misleading statement to form, one which

the fisher syndrome explained

---

appears to imply that Fisher is, despite appearances to the contrary, really a realist. So, in these sections, there is un-simplifying variation and contrast too; and there is conscious avoidance of any chronology (even the generic works are shuffled so as to display pointed-ness but not evident thematic or biographical continuity. This is surely why the first section begins with 'Wonders of Obligation', that classic account of Fisher's reluctantly associative art "We know that hereabouts / comes into being / the malted-milk brickwork" and its—understated for the most part—cultural values: "The things we make out of language / turn into common property. / To feel responsible / I put my poor footprint back in."

Fisher, "unsure … for certain", has stated in an interview that there is still such a thing as "honest scepticism". He said it in the hey-day of that post-modern scepticism which, since it multiplies doubt to infinity, haplessly drops scepticism out of the equation—allowing its proponents to flourish mechanical rejections of justifiable assertion (about what truth is, for instance) that in practice leaves everything precisely as it was. Honest scepticism, I take it, means allowing doubt its place in an understanding of the world, both natural and human. Doubt then functions as a means to further apprehension and understanding, not as a device for short-circuiting any such gains. Fisher has never believed, as Charles Tomlinson emblematically did with the title of his second collection, that "seeing is believing". He too has been, as he put it in 'City', a poet who lived "so much by the eye", but he did so to address the processes by which the world takes shape around us, breaking up, and reconfiguring its solidities, altering the angles of sight, or focal length, so as to access a knowledge of change and evolution. 'A Furnace' proceeds by enacting the life of energies, powers, forms, or evidences not only to access knowledge of change, but to assist it. Fisher's scepticism about poetry with a moral attached has found its role in defining his field of operations, since on its right flank were the social moralists of the 1950s, Philip Larkin, Kingsley Amis and Davie, with, nearby, in the Tomlinson of the 1960s and 1970s, an epistemological moralist of international distinction.

However, to live outside the law you must be honest; and Fisher's scepticism means that he is not without beliefs about aesthetic, literary, poetic, and therefore social and political conduct—beliefs that might be identified in the differences between overtly propagated rules of behaviour with a social flavour, and complexes of learned practices about relations with others that, for one thing, would be betrayed by imposing them on others, by boasting about holding them, or by announcing that you have just acted in accord with them. In 'The Lesson in Composition', Fisher writes of how "Whatever I start from / I go for the laws of its evolution, / de-socializing art, diffusing it / through the rest till there's no escaping it." This is a prosaic poem responding to the oppressive social demand that the marketplace has, mysteriously, imposed on poetry over the last few decades. I say "mysteriously" because you would have thought that the marketplace has so little real use for poetry, it not making much money for anyone, that it could have been left in peace. The thorough marginalization of the art some time before the rise of our current version of market economics should have found it well positioned to resist such demands. Yet such is the power of ideology that poetry's more socially adaptive operators have felt compelled to sing from the same stock-exchange hymn-sheet. Fisher's poem approaches its end by describing the British version of this problem. "Art talks", he writes,

> of its own processes, or talks about the rest
> in terms of the processes of art; or stunts itself
> to talk about the rest in the rest's own terms
> of crisis and false report—entertainment,
> that worldliness that sticks to me
> so much I get sent outside
> when the work wants to start.
>
> I'm old enough to want to be prosaic;
> I shall have my way.

Art offers its benefits to individuals and, through them, to the society at large, only if it is allowed to follow its processes without the imposition of formulated social demands—whether they are promulgated by a national union of writers, or as a requirement from publishers and their allies in newspapers and award bodies to address the immediate interests of imagined consumers. Fisher's scepticism about identity and the idea

the fisher syndrome explained

---

of the discontinuous self, the role of body sensations, of ontology in epistemology can also be related—paradoxically it might seem—to Jazz and the life of the performer.

Yet this is not pop music. Fisher became interested in his music at a point just before the moment when it was to be pushed aside. He has, as a consequence of that marginalization, accompanied distinguished American performers on their tours of the British provinces. This is slightly different from the kinds of relation to an audience of readers that many writers will take for granted. The latter is slower, more cumulative, based upon two separated activities that take place within the privacy of the writer's or reader's conscious minds—and one that is only supported, or sometimes even hindered, by encounters with the poet in performance. The musician who performs on a nightly basis needs an internalized sense of what a good performance will be that pays only marginal attention to what the audience may or may not have thought. Fisher is thus complexly placed both to understand the way in which art is necessarily a matter of presenting its products to informed people who appreciate that art, and of knowing how to preserve the autonomy of the performer from audience demands that can in so many ways prove to be art's ruination.

The doubt about being able to know ourselves, a first step on the road to such self-knowledge as may be granted us, naturally extends in honest sceptics to the knowledge of others. The limited access allowed to the rest of the world then requires a process of acquaintance, a repeated returning to and reconsidering of phenomena. One limit in Fisher's work is the locating of experience in shared relationships between people. The works that might seem at first most to qualify such a statement ('Interiors with Various Figures' and 'The Ship's Orchestra') only tend on closer acquaintance with their unique strangeness to reinforce it. This limit might seem to be escaped from by the comedy poems of section III. Comedy requires a relation to constituencies and social groups. The poet's relative lack of ease with such situations of identification and provision, may account for some of the weaknesses in that section. 'Sets', for instance, was inspired by the quarrels between various groups and sub-groups of poets about who precisely should control the UK Poetry Society. Beyond the more 'committed' inner circles of such writers and their support teams it might be expected to reverberate with rather less force:

Peter Robinson

> If you take a poem
> you must take another
> and another
> till you have a poet.
>
> And if you take a poet
> you'll take another, and so on,
> till finally you get
> a civilization: or just
> the dirtiest brawl you ever saw—
> the choice isn't yours.

What saves this from being a faded joke about a shrunken corner of a lost world, is the crispness and clarity not only of the writing, but also of the double disappointment it dramatizes through, for example, the workings of unobtrusive rhymes: "poet . . . get", "so on . . . civilization", and "saw . . . yours". Equally, the way that "or just" breaks up the resolving rhymed close on the word "civilization" is a perfectly judged ruffling of high-minded high hopes. So the poem first describes a process that we who admire and enjoy this art have all experienced—the growth of a learned and then fed fascination that can access some of the finest productions of highly sensitized minds, and then marks a precipitous slide into isolation, conflict, and the total loss of anything like art or control. Many of Fisher's poems dedicated to other poets could be called counteractive moves in this cultural destruction of poetry and the conditions for its best production. 'You Should Have Been There', written for Peter Riley in 2000, is exemplary in its acknowledgement of just how essential imaginative collaboration is in this most personal, and often most isolate, of arts: "you should have been there / to make two of our sort / too many for the territory / I'd split the shift with you", he proposes, "while the broad- / bodied waitress in black with an ominous eye / stalks by".

Roy Fisher's is, then, a poetry of scepticism, one that included a healthy scepticism of poetry. It has been protected from the cancelling to nothing of moralized minimalism—by accepting a need to grow loquacious and to address with ever greater reach the implications and ramifications of its congenial, not to say congenital, modes first

the fisher syndrome explained

---

intuited through exposure via Gael Turnbull to American writers such as W.C. Williams, Denise Levertov, and Cid Corman in the late 1950s and early 1960s. This is what Fisher's lesser known, and by some less appreciated, work of the 1980s and 1990s has been about. In 'A Furnace' and elsewhere his "honest scepticism" has tacitly defined a complex social and political agnosticism—addressing, for instance, the survival of ancient religious modes for giving significance to mortal processes, while criticizing established religion's expropriation of death, and the role of the dead in our lives. Since the end of the 1970s, Fisher has published work that takes carefully calibrated steps in the direction of the social, while simultaneously keeping the time's overweening social demands in their place. He has indeed put his "poor footprint back in". The first part of 'Texts for a Film' (1991) begins "Birmingham's what I think with" and over more than fifty years this poet has found evolving means for turning that thought into art. I first encountered his poetry on a library shelf some thirty-five ago. If not quite "what I think with", Roy Fisher's work has nonetheless contributed substantially to what and how I think—and, *al que quiere!* (to those who desire), it can do the same.

The two parts combined above are reprinted with some occasional local revision from Grosseteste Review 13, *1981, and* Notre Dame Review 22, *2006. While the first records a moment of critical distancing when, at the age of 28, I felt the need to grow away from the most abiding presence and influence on my way of thinking and writing, the latter is among recent efforts to acknowledge and pay tribute to the lifelong debts incurred.*

MATTHEW SPERLING

Water

1

As I sat down to write this piece, a message landed in my inbox inviting me to attend a lecture at the Institute of English Studies by Jonathan Bate, under the title 'The Poet and the River: Wordsworth, Coleridge, Hughes'. I didn't go along. In 2006 I heard Bate give a keynote talk in Oxford, and I have in front of me the "inaugural" issue of the journal associated with that conference, which calls itself, as the conference did, *British and Irish Contemporary Poetry*. The inaugural issue now appears to be also the only issue, since Liverpool University Press's website offers this 'Synopsis': "THIS JOURNAL HAS BEEN DISCONTINUED". There, under the title 'The Green Line in Contemporary Poetry', Bate rounds up a troupe of poets all doing a version of "contemporary ecological poetry": David Morley, Czesław Miłosz, Michael Longley, John Burnside, Glynn Maxwell, Johannes Bobrowski, Geoffrey Hill, Peter Redgrove, Alice Oswald, Kathleen Jamie, Peter Abbs ... As that line-up suggests, it's a hit and miss affair, but Bate's important point is that ecological writing is most worthwhile, as in Oswald's *Dart* (2002), when it "seems to engage with ecology as it now is in the political sense", "with a clear sense of the working life and the rural economy", "in which landscape is inseparable from labour". In case this version of "now" all sounds a bit nineteenth-century, Bate also has some flashier stuff from Bruno Latour's *We Have Never Been Modern* (1993), to illustrate the idea that "nature and culture are deeply imbricated", and exist as a "web of relations":

> The ozone hole is too social and too narrated to be truly natural; the strategy of industrial firms and heads of state is too full of chemical reactions to be reduced to power and interest; the discourse of the ecosphere is too real and too social to boil down to meaning effects. ... Where are we to put these hybrids? Are they human? Human because they are our work? Are they natural? Natural because they are not our doing? Are they local or global? Both.

the fisher syndrome explained

The poet and the river. Not having heard Bate's more recent lecture, nonetheless I want to suggest that Roy Fisher should be, not just included in such discussions of ecological poetry, but central to them, and that Bate is missing out on what could be the most important case for his own argument. Bate's mooted eco-poetry is always threatening to devolve into a rag-tag of any old poems with a bit of flora and fauna in them. But it seems to me that Fisher is one of the few poets whose work puts the social and the economic back into "eco" in a genuinely cogent way. If I were to write another article on Fisher, this might be the thesis: that Fisher on water, Fisher on the river, is the best starting point for thinking about contemporary ecological poetry:

> I want
> to remark formally, indeed
> stiffly, though not complaining,
> that the place where I was raised
> had no longer deference for water
> and little of it showing. The Rea,
> the city's first river,
> meagre and upon the streets;
> and the Tame
> wandering waste grounds,
> always behind
> some factory or fence. . . .
>
> If you get systematic,
> and follow power around, you arrive
> at a bedrock out of a book. . . .
>
> Believe the Book of Bedrocks,
> as, in the end, you must,
> and you evolve Book City, just
> as it evolved itself: rock, water,
> forest, settlers, trade. Then
> property, sewage, architects, poets. . . .

These living rivers
turgidly watered the fields, gave

drink; drove low-powered mills, shoved
the Soho Works into motion, collected waste

and foul waters. Gave way to steam,
collected sewage, factory poisons. Gave way

to clean Welsh water, kept on collecting
typhoid. Sank out of sight

under streets, highways, the back walls of workshops;
collected metals, chemicals, aquicides. Ceased

to draw lines that weren't cancelled or unwanted; became
drains, with no part in anybody's plan. . . .

Abstracted water, captive for a while,
becomes abstract, a proposition in hydraulics,

slops through lock-machines, goes level,
carries coal, parties, makes money,

slides back into Nature, used.

The kind of understanding that I have in mind was given a prose explicitness in an interview with John Kerrigan. Kerrigan asks, in the light of Fisher's shift from Birmingham to 'rural Derbyshire', 'I wonder why there's been no move to something like nature poetry, now that you're out in the fields? When are we going to have your poems about pike and hawks roosting?' And Fisher replies:

> I live on a picturesque lane driven down through his tenants' fields by the 16th century Duke of Rutland / Lancaster / somewhere else anyway—let's call it Normandy—to get the coal down from his pits on the moor 400 feet above. The

the fisher syndrome explained

---

house is on a field labelled at that time "The King's Piece of Glutton". Over the wall is a small herd of heifers bred from bulls imported as frozen embryos; they're isolated because of ringworm. The BSE incinerator's two villages away. The skyline up the road is being shipped off to underlie the second runway at Manchester Airport. Dow Low rears above us, and I'll take the dog for a walk along the edge of its Drop when I've finished this. I don't know if that's an answer.

There is, of course, no such world as the "natural" world, and no relations to it that are not, as the saying goes, "always-already" economic relations. Once we begin on 'The Poet and the River' we immediately need to admit settlers, trade, property, sewage, metals, chemicals, aquicides; all the money, all the livelihoods drawn off from and engendered by water. Including the livelihoods of poets. Admittedly, this does not take me very far in thinking through the question. But if I tried to think it through, Roy Fisher would be what I'd think with.

2

The numinousness of Roy Fisher's poetry seemed to be stalking me, for a while in the middle of this or the last decade (depending where we count from). I can't think about reading Fisher without also thinking about what was important during several recent periods of my life; and, in a lesser degree, but only slightly lesser, the reverse is true.

After I'd left university in 2003 I spent two months intently reading Fisher, while working twelve-hour shifts for cash in hand (five fifty an hour, not bad money), in a shop called The Bonsai Store at Bluewater, the enormous shopping centre in North West Kent. Following my nose along a trail from somewhere, I had been lead on to Fisher. I suspect that I may first have encountered his work in Sean O'Brien's anthology, *The Firebox* (1998). I must have had the feeling that this would be up my street—or, perhaps more accurately, had the feeling that I wanted to be the sort of person whose street this would be up. I had built up a little collection: *The Dow Low Drop* from Bloodaxe (1996), light blue with the Kitaj cover ("after Walter Benjamin"), and *Poems 1955–1987* from Oxford (1988)—not so good looking, though the eye on the front is nice—both of them bought from Amazon Marketplace sellers; and *Birmingham River*, also from Oxford (1994), close to the end of their days as a poetry publisher, my copy bought at Skoob Books in London with my friend Ed Meehan; and the Shearsman *Interviews through Time and Selected Prose* (2000), again off Amazon.

That last one, especially, feels like a treasure. I think it might be my favourite Fisher book; and some days I think it might be my favourite *book*. I once wrote, self-importantly (and self-importantly repeat), that this book was 'the most coherent and insightful account of a poetics and its relation to political and social circumstances by any post-war British poet', and I still think that's probably true; but the book has another, more personal value too. I seem to be disposed to encounter phases of a mental paralysis in which I perceive myself, in a quite literal way, not to be a linguistic person any more; to be radically insufficient, radically incapable of language or thought. C.S. Lewis—of all people—has a way of putting something similar that stuck with me, near the beginning of his cranky old book *Studies in Words* (1960):

> Prolonged thought *about* the words which we ordinarily use to think *with* can produce a momentary aphasia. I think it is to be welcomed.

Except, for me, the state doesn't need any especially prolonged thought, to be induced. It just happens, and I suddenly feel filleted, collapsible. *Interviews through Time*, anyway, since I first read it, has become one of my go-to books, one reliable way of trying to ease myself out of this state. The book, and much of Fisher's other work, seems to show thinking in action more honestly, and somehow more adequately, than almost anything else I've encountered. I feel when reading it, that this actually is *enough*; that you actually can approximate something like what might be truthfulness, just with the words and syntax you have to hand. And after a while I can start to, as it were, come back to the linguistic world myself. So that I might really say, "Roy Fisher's what I think with". And this does, of course, sometimes make it difficult to think *about* him, and is one reason why I'm not rushing to write that essay on water.

the fisher syndrome explained

Anyway, those two months working at the bonsai shop in 2003, age twenty-one, I think I hardly read anything else. Almost all Fisher, in a mood of great ardency and also great desperation, trying to work out whether I even wanted to like poetry any more, or ever did; and with just about everything else to work out too. My job at The Bonsai Store was to prune and water the trees, and try to sell them to people, working up a little patter of my own. We bought them cheap from a nursery in Holland, which bought them even cheaper from a place in China. In the downtime between sales, sitting out on an open-sided stall (the RMU, or Retail Merchandising Unit), lined with bonsai trees, in the middle of the arcade, with the noise pollution from the Virgin records store (since Zavvi, and since defunct) on one side, and the nose pollution of the Lush soap store on the other side, I would read a few pages of Fisher. *City* or *The Ship's Orchestra* or *A Furnace* or whatever. And then I'd have to stash the book back in the draw under the till if a customer or the boss, John Paulus, was coming. Sometimes a colleague would be nosey about what I was reading, and I'd try to share. Explaining to Kam, an eighteen year-old school-leaver who said he didn't like reading, what was going on: *It's a sort of surrealist thing . . . like, there's this bit where this white suit with an orange for a head just walks in, as if it's just normal . . . it's all well mad.* And then recoiling into self-hurt at how lame it, and I, seemed to seem to Kam. As if Bluewater needed the surreal anyway. We practically all had citrus heads, in those days.

Flash forward two years. By which time I was back at university, and about to get married in a village called Hassop in Derbyshire, and happened just then to be writing an essay about the artist's books that Fisher collaborated on with Ronald King at the Circle Press. I needed a topic for a compulsory bibliography and text theory element on the Master's course I was doing, so I chased down the enticing entries in Derek Slade's bibliography, most of which, it seemed, had never been seen by critics. And then I spent some of the best days in libraries I've ever spent, and one day at the Circle Press's base in Notting Hill, looking at, and playing with, *Bluebeard's Castle*, and *The Left-Handed Punch*, and *Anansi Company*, and *Tabernacle*. Astonishing works. And then, after I had written an essay about these artist's books, in my gauche sort of way I sent Fisher an email, and I must have mentioned that I was knocking around in North Staffs, and he wrote back:

Matthew Sperling

> I pass by Hassop Hall quite frequently. Next time you're in Leek go up and take the crooked road off the A53 behind Ramshaw Rocks and you'll find Eleven Steps, which was my house when I wrote *A Furnace*.

I never did it. Can't drive, didn't want to put people out of their way, and so on. But somehow it didn't surprise me, that this place where I was about to get married was also a place in Roy Fisher's world.

Shortly after that, I was given a copy of the Fisher and Tom Phillips print 'Metamorphoses' as a Christmas present, quite out of the blue, and I have it here above my desk now. And shortly after that I found myself moving, less than a year later, and for one reason or another, to Birmingham, knowing more about the city from Fisher's poems than I did from the life. I had only been there maybe twice. I did a fair bit of mooching around imagining myself to be in a Roy Fisher poem; I was pleased to note that one of the local pubs was The Fighting Cocks, like on the first page of *A Furnace*. But I was living not in Fisher's Handsworth but in posh Moseley, in an 1930s art-deco building called Pitmaston Court, originally designed to accommodate the workers of the Ideal Insurance Group, who had a matching office building just round the corner, but now sold off to a private development company called Grainger, and turned into swish flats, with the slogan, "Country Living in the Heart of the City". The matching office building, Pitmaston House, was sold off in 2008 to be the Church of Scientology's Birmingham HQ. Cannon Hill Park, at the edge of which the River Rea ran ("meagre . . . wandering waste grounds"), was just out the back, behind the allotments, and Joe Chamberlain's Highbury Park (*rus in urbe*), named for his North London childhood, was equally close, on the way to King's Heath. In the meantime, my old essay on Fisher and Ron King got turned into an article which, with the peer-review process being what it is, and my life being what it was, was eventually published just around the time that everything fell apart, and I gave up on being married, and left Birmingham.

And it strikes me that for most of this time—these several years—I didn't really know anybody else who was a reader of Roy Fisher. Except for myself. I'd never had much of a conversation with anyone about Fisher. There was something strange and inward and deflected and

the fisher syndrome explained

---

private about it, and in a way there still is. When *PN Review* asked me to write about *The Long and the Short of It*, the request came out of the blue, and presumably, from their side, utterly on spec. I didn't think they knew anything about me! It spooked me a bit, that the first book they asked me to review was Roy Fisher. This was new, this was strange, trying to make public something that I quite liked to be private. I realise now that when I wrote, above, that I had "the feeling that I wanted to be the sort of person whose street Fisher's poetry would be up", I was imagining myself to be stealing a construction from Fisher himself—from the remarkable moment in his 'Antebiography' where he writes: "I came to feel, as I turned nineteen, that I ought to want to write. I seemed to be becoming the sort of young man who had that ambition". Similarly, I spent a long time in the last few years trying to write a novel, which I'd like to be able to finish one day, but it's absolutely full, I realise, of phrases taken straight from Fisher. I can't quite tell that I didn't write them myself.

I met John Kerrigan, years later, when he came to do a paper on MacNiece at an Irish Literature seminar my friends Tom and Sarah ran, and we spoke briefly afterwards, and I guess I'd been thinking beforehand, *Ah, we can talk about Roy Fisher*. But he asked me what I was working on, and I told him the subject of my doctorate, and Kerrigan looked a bit bored and said, *Well, that sounds like a barrel of laughs*, and then he told me what I should be doing instead: reading Roy Fisher. And what I should have said is, *I've been doing it for seven years already*, but I wasn't in the mood, and so I let it slide. My secret, then.

A blurbish sentence for the end. I want to remark formally, indeed stiffly, that Roy Fisher's poetry is too social and too narrated to be truly natural, too full of chemical reactions to be reduced to power and interest, too real to boil down to meaning effects; and that this work taken as a whole is some of the most human, the most local and global being made in Britain today.

SUE STANFORD

The Seat of his Pants

In 1963 Roy left one College of Education and took promotion in another. At the time of his appointment as Principal Lecturer in English it was to a Birmingham Temporary Day College of Education not yet in existence. It was a daring step to take. If an insufficient number of women applied to train as primary school teachers (it was to be a women-only college) then the place would never open. It was a precarious venture that Roy was joining but the challenge outweighed the risk.

Mrs Delphine Roe, the principal, came seconded from the local inspectorate and was all too aware of the shortage of qualified primary school teachers. She brought with her an almost Sicilian grasp of the strengths and weaknesses within primary education in Birmingham and was able to pick inspired teachers to join her team so that when the college opened, as Bordesley College of Education, of the seven members of staff only three had ever worked in a college before. A lot of responsibility fell on those three. Mrs Roe was enthusiastic and confident and though at times she might need to be reined in she knew exactly what made a good teacher.

The college premises were half of King Edward VI Grammar School for Boys, Camp Hill, one of the five King Edward's schools in Birmingham, but in decline. It was running out of boys and was due to close in a couple of years. A Victorian building standing at the corner of a complex junction at the top of the Stratford Road, noisy and fumy and not a blade of grass in sight.

When I took up a post in the education department of the college in 1965 there was no longer any precariousness. The first batch of students had nearly completed their three-year training, and they were already being promised jobs, often by the schools they had visited for their teaching practice. The grammar school had closed and Bordesley College occupied the whole site. The majority of the students were mature women whose education had been disrupted, some by the war and some by marriage and families. A frightening number had been teaching, totally unqualified, since the view at the time was, as Roy put it, that anyone who could run a children's party without casualties was capable of taking charge of a class of 40 five-year-olds and teaching them to read.

the fisher syndrome explained

The strength of the college lay in the quality of the teaching that the students received in the specialist subjects and also in the supervision of their teaching practice. The English department had expanded and Roy now had five or six lecturers in his team, often adding to rather than easing his workload. The students were hungry to learn but with no common background in the subject the policy was that they all had individual programmes of work designed for them, not always covered by their tutor's reading. Roy speaks of the seat of his pants.

All the lecturers at every level took part in supervising teaching practice. We worked in teams and each member was responsible for five or six students who we visited every week of a term-long placement in a school. Sitting unobtrusively on a child's chair at the back of a classroom we would make notes in a duplicate book on what we saw, tearing off the top copy to leave in the student's folder and keeping the carbon for Friday when all the students who were on teaching practice came into college for a tutorial. Away from the school it was easier to reflect on why a lesson had been successful, or what might be done if it hadn't. This wasn't simply learning by doing and somehow getting the hang of it in the end, it was guided questioning of the whole process of teaching and learning; all the lecturers had been classroom teachers who knew what they were talking about.

We were equipping the students for a new career and nearly all of them were keen to do whatever it took to become teachers. Attracta McCrudden, Concepta O'Shaughnessy, Avril Shufflebottom, Verity Mundy and those other fine women who were to enrich the primary schools of Birmingham made us feel we were doing a good job.

In those days Roy was slender, hair-topped. His navy blue, double breasted suit, the seat slightly shiny and jacket unbuttoned, gave the message that he knew what he was meant to do but that he might do something quite different. I learnt Birmingham from him. And the poetry? He kept that in another compartment. Someone must have told me because when I read in *The Listener* or the *New Statesman* that Roy Fisher was the most underrated poet writing in Britain then, I thought I would leave that to others and stick with the Roy I knew.

JEFFREY WAINWRIGHT

'Art's Marvellous'

Asked to characterise his perfect reader Roy Fisher told John Kerrigan that "she would be a woman who would nose around the back of a row of lockup garages to see what she could see, without making a song and dance about it". Nosing about the index of Fisher's *The Long and the Short of It, Poems 1955–2005*, she might happen upon two poems entitled 'The Square House, February', and 'The Square House, April'. Both dated at 1982, they must seem contiguous but in this volume they are actually placed some fifty pages apart, indeed in different sections. Both poems are "views", the first of a snowfall, the second of the movements of birds. But in both poems, although the evocations are beautifully realised, it is the nature of the "viewing" that is most arresting.

In 'February' the house's "neat / wide windows framed in white / idly take pictures of the weather" and these only appear to the speaker "over my shoulder or / out of the corner of my eye". The scene is before us now because it was watched, but the sense that its recording was automatic increases the obvious sense that the fall is happening anyway and, at the end of the poem, "will do that for most / of a dark afternoon / settling hardly at all". This leaves the person aside, separated not only from Nature, however precisely it can be instanced as coming "into Staffordshire / by way of the Cheshire Gap and Crewe", but from his own poem. By 'April' there is a different self. The birds are about their own purposes and exactly described—"the single magpie / hung like a parrot tail-heavy / in the sycamore"—but again it is not the "view" that is really what is seen.

> There's something in the fluid air
> something in nothing
> in the null
> middle of the day
>
> They are in it and I
> witness it.

the fisher syndrome explained

Now the viewer is clearly before us with a distinct, perhaps alienated, sense of difference from Nature. The description continues with a touch more urgency as "the finches are jumping like / lice among the bushes" until the poem ends:

> the rooks marshal and manoeuvre
> in the something they sense.
> They are in it. I
> witness it. It is in
> me.

In both poems the views from "the square house", for all that its designation seems so set and solid, are anything but fixed. At one moment here is the view without the viewer; then a "sense" that there is more here than is obviously before us—"something in nothing"; then, in the deliberately awkward jerkiness of the closing rhythms of 'April', the nearly mystical realisation that through the act of witness that which is outside suffuses the self. Typically, in the process of these unassuming short poems of such seemingly local ambition, we are brought to see "something in nothing".

Seeing "something in nothing" is usually an accusation, and this counter-suggestion is not absent from Fisher's use of the phrase here. I may also seem to be making a song and dance about just two poems in all but a life's work. But Fisher imagines, and indeed trains a reader to expect interest from unlikely corners and I think they can be taken as indicative. First their wide separation, occupied by poems both much earlier and later in composition, points up the principles of the composition of this Collected, and shows in turn how poorly our more consecutive, linear conceptions describe Roy Fisher's cast of mind. In the briefest of introductory notes to the volume, at the end of the Acknowledgements, Fisher writes: "These poems no more amount to a biography than I do" and that his working methods over time "would make an arrangement that seemed chronological false". There can be very many pages between 'February' and 'April'.

The Long and the Short of It is organised to show the different types of Fisher's poetry. The opening section comprises his major sequences, 'City', 'A Furnace', 'The Cut Pages', 'The Ship's Orchestra' and the major longer poems 'Wonders of Obligation' and 'The Dow Low Drop'. At the opposite end of the book other sections include collaborations such as his 'Texts for a Film', written for Tom Pickard's superb film on Fisher and Birmingham, and 'Inscriptions for Bluebeard's Castle'. The third section collects Fisher's hilarious satirical poems, mostly aimed at various aspects of the contemporary poetry business. 'The Poetry Promise': "We are committed to progressive reduction of the time it takes the penny to drop after you finish reading a poem"; that "All our poems are at the very least relevant", and "will be written in guidelines", is at once a deadly parody of today's successful poem, of the folly of bureaucratic mission statements, and an anti-description of a Fisher poem. His non-delivery on the promise probably accounts for his routine failure to arrive into the annual prize lists. The other sections, mostly of shorter individual poems, are less clearly delineated, and best suited to nosing about.

The second reason why I take the 'Square House' poems to be indicative is that unremarkable character of their setting and occasions. The Sublime is not Roy Fisher's scene. He is not smitten by the Simplon Pass but "obsessed / with cambered tarmacs, concretes, / the washings of rain" ('Wonders of Obligation'). He describes the nondescript:

> When the far bank darkens
> and the river starts to die
> the nondescript
> silently fights for its life   ('The Dow Low Drop')

There is always something even more common-or-garden:

> Beyond that, the track
> baffles, turns into nothing or anything,
>
> but best, at the bottom of the wood
> a field-gate chained shut
> and an unmarked meadow   ('Near Garmsley Camp')

Such an enthusiasm—"but best"—is surely why he found William Carlos Williams' work such a companion early in his career. The

the fisher syndrome explained

---

pretensions of centres, advertised focal points are anathema to him. Perhaps paradoxically, it is this that makes him so distinctive as a poet of cities. The classical image of the city is radiant, its centre at once a symbolic or actual culmination of its energies and a distributor of the enlightenment it has gathered. This was the vision of the 18th century industrial captains and visionaries of the Midlands such as Matthew Boulton and Josiah Wedgwood. But Fisher's Birmingham, unnamed as yet but the locus of 'City', whose first version appeared in 1961, appears first in demolition, its streets "rough quadrilaterals of brick rubble, veering awkwardly towards one another through nothing". It is recurrently marginal, as though still oscillating between country and town, nature and culture. Under the impact of what apologists describe as the 'creative destruction' of capitalism, and of war, Fisher's generation has seen the "built environment" of its swathes of mass-housing and vast industrial installations become decrepit or be swept away. When I first read 'City' and the poems in *The Memorial Fountain* in the 1960s, besides recognising and welcoming an anti-pastoralism, I took the poems to be taking the modern city and its life as a solid subject with a history and a present to relate. Here was "Lucas's / lamp factory", a man pissing in a corner "straddling to keep his shoes dry": real life. What I did not see was Fisher's frame round this, that that poem is called 'For Realism' and thus that its relation to its material is oblique and self-aware. These poems, like their great successors, 'Wonders of Obligation' and 'A Furnace', are "social", but their deeper subject is change, flux and instability. This is how Fisher describes "the field I was born in":

> long slope of scrub, then pasture,
> still blank on the map three hundred years
> after the walkings of all such gentlemen
> out of the air
>
> then suddenly printed across with
> this century, new, a single
> passage of the roller
> dealing out streets of terraces
> that map like ratchet-strips, their gables
> gazing in ranks above the gardens
> at a factory sportsground,

>   a water-tower for steam-cranes, more
>   worksheds, and,
>   hulking along a bank
>   for a sunset peristyle, the long dark
>   tunnel-top roof of a football stadium.
>   (II 'The Return')

And then, as 'City' describes, it is gone again. "I seem to have been born", Fisher tells Kerrigan, "swimming in Mutability". Later he describes his childhood "neighbour-fear", the old couple next door and their demented dog, a "dung-coloured whirl of hatred", the

>   Slow-dying woman,
>   her life was primordial and total,
>   the gaze-back of the ikon; her death
>   modern and nothing, a weekend in the Cold War.
>   The dog must have brained itself.
>   (III 'Authorities')

This swim is modernity. It consumes, changes, making people in that chilling phrase, "modern and nothing". As we can see much more clearly now, Fisher's acute sense of and concentration upon the underlying processes of mutability was the really deep perception about the "reality" of the twentieth century, in its cities and elsewhere: the relentless consumption, destruction and change that is key to the capitalist process.

The next lines in that passage about the neighbours begin, "Had the three of them been art . . ." What, we might ask, has art to do with this? For Fisher, everything. The sensibility that looks at nondescript detail and is so convinced of evanescence and a multiplicity of seeings recognises the reality of artistic practice, verbal, musical and visual. Here, in 'Wonders of Obligation', he describes "the first farmyard I ever saw / . . . mostly midden / a collapse of black / with dung and straw swirls". Then

>   The other farm I had
>   was in an old picture book,
>   deep-tinted idyll with steam

the fisher syndrome explained

> threshers, laughing men,
> Bruno the hound with his black muzzle,
> and the World's Tabbiest Cat.

To describe the first, he continues, "moralises it; as the other always was" and he goes on:

> But I swear
> I saw them both then
> in all their properties,
> and to me, the difference was neutral.

The nature of the mind, we realise, is that its realities are multiple. Only Authority seeks to impose unity that is the topic of the third, 'Authorities' section of 'A Furnace'. The half-understood, ill-taught grand theories such as Whig history do not fit, and even less

> did the history of class struggle
> reach down or along to the working-
> class streets where work and wages
> hid, as the most real shame[.]

The neurotic petty suspicions and enmities of the "feared neighbours" allowed little for solidarity. No single vision encompasses all this, as Fisher knew early on in this prose passage from 'City':

> I want to believe I live in a single world. That is why I am keeping my eyes at home while I can. The light keeps on separating the world like a table knife: it sweeps across what I see and suggests what I do not. The imaginary comes to me with as much force as the real, the remembered with as much force as the immediate. The countries on the map pile up like ice-floes: what is strange is that I feel no stress, no grating discomfort among the confusion, no loss; only a belief that I should not be here. I see the iron fences and the shallow ditches of the countryside the mild wind has travelled over. I cannot enter that countryside; nor can I escape it. I cannot join together the mild wind and the shallow ditches, I cannot

lay the light across the world and then watch it slide away. Each thought is at once translucent and icily capricious. A polytheism without gods.

This section of 'City', 'The Wind at Night', seems to me profoundly important for Fisher's work as a whole. Moving from verse to prose he is "walking through the suburb at night . . . I pass . . . I stare . . . I sense . . . I see . . ." and

> I have often felt myself to be vicious, in living so much by the eye, yet among so many people. I can be afraid that the egg of light through which I see these bodies might present itself as a keyhole. Yet I can find no sadism in the way I see them now.

Nor is there in his sketches of people ever any sense of "sadism". But in these passages he is scrutinising his own sensibility. He shows us the actuality of when "the imaginary comes to me with as much force as the real", and the exhilaration it can bring: "I come quite often now upon a sort of ecstasy, a rag of light blowing among things I know". Yet it also brings "a belief that I should not be here . . . Each thought is at once translucent and icily capricious."

To explore this caprice further let's move from the city to a plant pot. This is the whole of 'The Only Image' (1975):

> Salts work their way
> to the outside of a plant pot
> and dry white.
>
>   This encrustation
> is the only image.
>   The rest —
> the entire winter, if there's winter —
> comes as a variable that shifts
> in any part, or vanishes.
>
>   I can
> compare what I like to the salts,

the fisher syndrome explained

>   to the pot, if there's a pot,
>   to the winter if there's a winter.
>
>   The salts I can compare
>   to anything there is.
>   Anything.

The syntactic inversion in the last two paragraphs—"I can / compare . . . the salts . . . The salts I can compare"—effect a rising emphatic rhythm which, with the extravagant "Anything", becomes heady with the notion of imaginative freedom. There is a touch of pugnacity too: look, this is what I can get out of the blotches on a plant pot! But doesn't the hyperbole also admit the possibility of caprice? It will be no coincidence that the following poem in the volume, *The Memorial Fountain* (1965), ends with a man "by temper, realist . . . working / to distinguish an event / from an opinion", and has the final phrase "Romantic notion". Nevertheless, it will be in the nature of the imagination to be euphoric as it carries into the forms of art. The previous poem is Fisher's homage to the jazz pianist Joe Sullivan and concludes:

>   And that thing is his mood
>   a feeling violent and ordinary
>
>   that runs in among standard forms so
>   wrapped up in clarity
>
>   that fingers that following his
>   through figures that sound obvious
>
>   find corners everywhere,
>   marks of invention, wakefulness;
>
>   the rapid and perverse
>   tracks that ordinary feelings
>
>   make when they get driven
>   hard enough against time.

Here "time" is the form of the art and it may produce the perverse but also "marks of invention, wakefulness".

This is the moment to say something about Fisher's own running "in among standard forms". The poems lately referred to, drawn from a wide chronological spread, also exemplify most of Fisher's most characteristic formal procedures: for instance the movements between verse and prose in 'City', different dispositions of free verse lines in the pairings of 'The Thing About Joe Sullivan' and 'The Only Image', and a wider use of the page in 'The Memorial Fountain'. What they all show is the absolute appropriateness of Fisher's free verse methods to his material. In his 'Antebiography' he writes of how his discovery of American modernism, especially the Black Mountain group, released his work so that "I could get at observations, memories, earlier selves, lost feelings, casual things—reality in short—and my clotted language cleared like a cloudy liquid left to settle." These writers "were behaving with all the freedom and artistic optimism of painters. Decidedly un-English." He adapts American practice to his own purposes without playing American in any style. What free verse and open field composition allows is the elements of occurrence, notation, immediacy, improvisation, lightness and mobility in his perceptions to be represented. The impressionist inheritance of modernism—in poetry as in painting—permits the significant to emerge from the unassuming, the nondescript to "fight for its life". Consequently the multiplicity of vision, collage, "juxtaposition with science" as Pound called it, of modernist practice enable a voice which never felt comfortable with pronouncement and always pauses before eloquence. It fits too the modern versions of change and decay, wry and fleet-footed enough to stay true to impressions and avoid the consumerism of advanced capitalist culture. He has evolved a polymorphous style to catch those shifting, protean thoughts. A monologic—indeed monotheistic—disposition will not catch them:

> One particular of Poseidon: the bronze statue
> through whose emptied eyeholes
> entire Poseidon comes and goes.
>
> ('A Furnace', VI 'The Many')

the fisher syndrome explained

His "polytheism without gods" admits variations of tone in which the comedy straight-man's brand of delivery is never far away: "There have always been / saucers put out for us / by the gods."

Presumably these saucers keep us going, and putting them out is a quiet almost hidden act, lacking all godly flourish, and the opposite of laying down tablets of stone. Perhaps they are like that "rag of light" that brings ecstasy; like "that body of air" between ceiling and cupboard-top "that's like / nothing that ever was"; that "field-gate chained shut" and the meadow "floating a foot above its own grassy floor". These things materialise through art, and it is the art already existing which helps us to see them, even 'In the Black Country': "Dudley from the Castle keep / looks like a town by Kokoschka," thus offering "plural perspectives", "landscapes of opportunity", "a selection of skies", which is why, as the poem concludes, "Art's marvellous." But this is not a godly world. Above the field-gate and meadow of 'Near Garmsley Camp',

> visible for miles
> a man stands sunlit and hammering
> high on Edvyn Loach church steeple,
> trespassing in the air claimed for spirits
> by the stone push upwards, and giving
> the game away; an entire man standing
> upright in the sky.

Art is work and Fisher's work shows us our complex world. This image of the steeplejack is unusually fixed and available to interpretation, but there again is the straight-man's note: "giving the game away", and the image stays in motion, "hammering".

Notes

This essay was first published as a review of Roy Fisher, *The Long and the Short of It: Poems 1955–2005* (Bloodaxe Books, 2005) in *Stand*, vol. 7 no. 2, 2007. The interview with John Kerrigan, 'Come to Think of It, the Imagination', is to be found in *News for the Ear: A Homage to Roy Fisher* eds. Robert Sheppard and Peter Robinson, (Stride, 2000). Roy Fisher's 'Antebiography' is in *Interviews Through Time and Selected Prose* (Shearsman Books, 2000).

DAVID WHEATLEY

The Secret Laugh of the World

1

As gestures go, publishing a *Collected Poems* before you turn forty would seem to be on the grandiose side, but when Roy Fisher (b. 1930) published his in 1969 he hadn't been writing for several years and wasn't expecting to again. What readers might have thought was a smirk on his face was in reality closer to a valedictory grimace. *Collected Poems* came with a jacket photograph of a young boy at a street party in Birmingham for George V's silver jubilee. The scene is straight from a poem like 'Toyland', with its "old couples, the widowed, the staunch smilers, / The deprived and the few nubile young lily-ladies." One youngster doesn't look very impressed with his plate of biscuits either, and unlike most of the other revellers hasn't bothered to put his paper hat on. A sharp-eyed observer might diagnose a case of proleptic post-imperial ennui, as the crowd waits for the barbarians at the gate who, even in 1935, must have been looking like "a kind of solution", as Cavafy would put it. Fisher's classmates, after all, express a "half-shocked envy" when his aunt and two cousins are blown up in a bombing raid a few years later. As for Fisher himself, he has never been one for nostalgia: "I had no pain of it; can find no scar even now". Philip Larkin does a good job of blanking out wartime Coventry in 'I Remember, I Remember', but not before he had permitted himself the wistfulness of 'The March Past' and its "astonishing remorse for things now ended / That of themselves were also rich and splendid /(But unsupported broke, and were not mended)". Fisher's un-astonished blankness in the face of the national question, by contrast, is consistently unflinching. In 'The Nation' he describes a "national day" on which everything described is prefaced by the adjective "national", reducing the concept to a state of pleonastic exhaustion long before a group of offenders are clapped in the "national prison" and subjected to the "national /method of execution" for succumbing to the "national vice", whatever that might be.

Organising a nationwide party to mark the occasion might be a bit excessive, but readers sitting down to Fisher's work for the first time would have every right to feel in celebratory mood. Why wouldn't they?

the fisher syndrome explained

He's one of the best English writers around. Yet for all the superlatives I may wish to throw in his direction, Fisher's position in British poetry today is an uneasy one. A lot of his books are hard to find or long out of print. Sometimes his anthology number comes up, but sometimes it doesn't. Like Philip Larkin he loves Pee-Wee Russell and Coleman Hawkins, but unlike Larkin he also likes the Black Mountain Poets and has been known to call himself "a 1905 Russian Modernist", which suggests that membership of the "old-type natural fouled-up guys" club will forever elude him. Though held in great esteem by admirers—as witness the festschrift, *News for the Ear*, and John Kerrigan and Peter Robinson's essay collection *The Thing About Roy Fisher*—he has never quite loomed large enough in the landscape for the readership he needs and deserves. There was a Fisher *Collected Poems* in 1969 but there wasn't as recently as 2004, before the appearance of *The Long and the Short of It: Poems 1955–2005*, and if that isn't a textbook definition of the phrase 'arsy-versy' I don't know what is.

Fisher's first book, *City*, appeared in 1961. Robert Conquest's Movement anthology, *New Lines*, was still policing sphincters up and down the land, but foreign help was at hand the following year in the form of Alvarez's *The New Poetry*. The names on the team sheet were Lowell, Berryman, Plath and Sexton. If only things had been that simple! The delicious irony of *The New Poetry* was that, for an anthology so concerned to blast British poetry out of its "gentility principle", Alvarez fell prey to an American gentility principle of his own, suppressing any suggestion that the American poetry of the 60s might also stretch to Ginsberg, Duncan, O'Hara, Schuyler, Rakosi, Oppen, Dorn, Niedecker or Spicer. Any writers under their influence on this side of the water were thus doubly excluded. A crucial conduit of alternative American writing in Britain was Fulcrum Press, publisher of Fisher's study in itchy paranoia *The Ship's Orchestra*, *Collected Poems* and *Matrix*, and most unusually of all the books I want to discuss here, *The Cut Pages*. Sketched as an attempt to shake off a long spell of writer's block, this is still the most extreme of his books and to some critics (notably Marjorie Perloff) his truest and best. Discontinuity is all—freedom from what Beckett called "the vulgarity of a plausible concatenation". As Fisher puts it in an author's note, the aim was "to give the words as much relief as possible from serving in planned situations; so the work

David Wheatley

was taken forward with no programme beyond the principle that it should not know where its next meal was coming from."

Before turning to *The Cut Pages* I would like to propose the phrase "Tennis Court Oath syndrome" as a contribution to literary discourse. Tennis Court Oath syndrome is what happens when readers think they've worked out something startling and new, only for the writer to turn around and trump them with something not just startlingly new but incomprehensibly so, even and precisely at the risk of alienating his or her greatest admirers. Since I'm naming it after his notorious second book, John Ashbery displays Tennis Court Oath syndrome, or did once, a very long time ago. But sooner or later all writers have to decide where they stand on the innovation question. Some make it the driving force of their careers, turning from the "plane of the feasible" in disgust, as Beckett urged Duthuit, "weary of pretending to be able, of being able, of doing a little better the same old thing, of going a little further along a dreary road"; others would have us believe that "All we can do is write on the old themes in the old styles, but try to do a little better than those who went before us", as Hardy told Robert Graves. To describe *The Cut Pages* as a case of Tennis Court Oath syndrome, coming as it does after the not exactly easy reading of *The Ship's Orchestra*, is to underline just how extreme a departure it was. But Fisher has never innovated for innovation's sake or because he expects a congratulatory telegram from the academy of fine ideas: the dust jacket of *The Cut Pages* warns that "he should not be categorised as an 'experimental prose writer'", and "does not fit any of the familiar formulae of modernism." If they were familiar, they'd hardly be any use anyway. The motivating force behind *The Cut Pages* was more urgently personal and painful than that.

To start with the title: the pages are "cut" because, keeping a "diary of demoralisation" during his writer's block, Fisher tired of having to skim past the old entries, so he tore out the blank pages and started again. Even so, the diary-like "entries in their hundreds" that followed this fresh start were "oblique, coded, desperate and dispiriting." The resulting book is 80 pages long, and divided into five sections: 'Metamorphoses', 'The Cut Pages', 'Stopped Frames and Set-Pieces', 'Hallucinations' and 'The Flight Orator'. The opening note describes the 'Metamorphoses' as "exercises in changing, in full view, one thing into another whose nature was quite unforeseen at the outset". Where elsewhere in the book Fisher pares his language down to miniature stumps and shells of sentences, here he delivers a hypnotic superabundance of detail that makes the language swim before the reader's eyes. In the first metamorphosis he describes a sleeping woman who changes into a swimmer, perhaps the swimmer we find in the first of the 'Stopped Frames and Set-Pieces' (and on the un-credited cover painting). The language sins against the Low Church modernist style-sheet in its unabashed embrace of metaphor:

> Enough depth. To clear and come free. There is no taste in the water, there are no edges under it: falling away, the soft mumbled hollows and mounds of marble, veined with brown, a lobby floor gone down into the descending levels of a sea-basin. The sleep comes naked
>
> Rising through the clear fluid, making their own way, the dragging wisps of brown that were secret hairs or the frame of a print on the wall. And light that cracks into the bubbles near the surface, lighting them like varnish bubbles, breaking them into the silent space between the surface and the curved roof, threaded with moving reflections of water light.

In the absence of any controlling narrative voice, the metaphoric transformations threaten to overwhelm rather than reassure the reader, building into a "mass of things, indistinguishable one from another". Information throws itself at the text faster than Fisher can process it: a man is "making for the ferry; no he's not. He stands a while and goes somewhere else." For all their morphing minute particulars, one thing the metamorphoses refuse to mutate into is a worldview: "No system describes the world". But this is not to license a return to self-sufficient empiricism. As Fisher observed of William Carlos Williams's famous dictum, "The trouble with 'No ideas but in things' is that it has become an idea." Unlike Williams, whose red wheelbarrow means just that, a red wheelbarrow, Fisher gives the impression of unmooring his objects to wander as they please. They are "dying to get out" and "exposed to the open at all events". The chain of metaphoric substitution in the visual field responds to and shapes an urban environment in constant destructive evolution: "Washes of screen. Men are fluttered. Houses are being thrown away wholesale. Butchers are on air."

The description of a man undressing in the fifth and final metamorphosis prepares us nicely for the stripping away of the narrative exoskeleton in the book's titular central section. One sure way to misrepresent 'The Cut Pages' would be to quote it within a prose paragraph like this, rather than on its own visual terms: if its atomised elements mean anything, it is in conjunction with the white space that separates them, much like the pauses for breath between "versets" in Beckett's *How It Is*. Each fragment establishes and is as suddenly forced to relinquish its hard-won textual space. What drives the text onwards so relentlessly, snatching the ground from under its feet? Fisher isn't saying. "There is no process" but "There are many changes". Attempting to make sense of this densely resistant writing Perloff has suggested that the sequence is organised around "three sets of verbal clusters: (1) references to ordering, control, containment; (2) references to movement, change, opening, journeying; and (3) images of vision and items that obscure vision—shade, shadow, shutter." In support of this we can point to Fisher's reliance on (dis)orienting terms such as "frame", "frameless", "cut", "origin", "displaced", "discontinuity", "undifferentiated" and "process", as the text ceaselessly changes perspective, attempting to bring into focus the experience of flux itself. When Donald Davie made his strenuous effort in *Thomas Hardy and British Poetry* to align Fisher with Larkin as a poet of rooted nostalgia for post-industrial Britain, he was forced to turn a blind eye to the jump cuts and discontinuities in Fisher's work; but, to do him justice, even in the forbidding atmosphere of *The Cut Pages* the language of rootedness and community mysteriously persists:

> Leviathan Lane. Home of the Works. Appears to have rolled over and huge stretches of its ghastly grey underparts come into view
>
> Stern of a spiral stair depending through glass light, in going down, in confined but neatly stacked office and reception space

the fisher syndrome explained

There is one flung out. On that one the light is sharp. There is no half-light; only the grace of diffusing what is full

They try to get in through the frosted glass, their spidery dark hands show almost visible as themselves as they scrabble. They come only at one oblique off-centre place; they can't succeed

Accretions after origin. Atypical hazard. All we are worrying about is our own distress at their frustration

Communitas. On the march. March a path to march on

I owned a patch, they marched on it. What march is that? My tit

Here is the "dispirited avoidance of concept, copula, cognition" which Simon Jarvis has found in Fisher at his most extreme, but as Fisher insists "This discontinuity is my discontinuity", not just any old statement of an abstract predicament. The obsession with lighting effects stages a series of theatrical spaces from which any actors have gone maddeningly absent ("Nobody has to have a face. Nobody who has a face can keep it.") The "they" are the off-stage prompters, town planners and literary aldermen laying down the city boundaries to which our urban and poetic narratives are expected to adhere. Fisher's repeated acts of cutting into his urban and narrative space allow him to find a fissure (the Fisher fissure) in these continuities and lose himself down it, White Rabbit-style. Or as he says in section three, "so much isn't the railroad, so little is." Another useful insight from Perloff is her comparison of the fourteen sections of this central sequence to the fourteen lines of a sonnet. The complaint that this writing is formless and sprawling has no foundation whatever; it's just that, as with the mystical urban geometry of *A Furnace*, the patterns are taking place over lengths beyond the visible limits of the two pages open before us. Stand on the Cerne Abbas man and you may notice that the earth beneath your feet is all chalky white, and nothing more; if you want to see the Cerne Abbas man you'll have to go and stand on the hill opposite instead. Trying to get the patterns of *The Cut Pages* into focus demands much the same effort.

The 1987 reprint of *The Cut Pages* contains only the central sequence, which leaves its relation to the original other four sections in some doubt. My preference is to see them as analogous to the 'Addenda' to Beckett's *Watt*, whose "precious and illuminating material should be carefully studied. Only fatigue and disgust prevented its incorporation." Particularly attractive is the description from 'Hallucinations' of the tombstone maker's yard and the discarded trunks of statues littering it. Here we confront not just a graveyard of possibilities, but a graveyard's graveyard. The albino raven Fisher finds there is emblematic of aborted promise, reminding the poet how "There are suburbs I have never properly visited, or have never managed to find recognisable as I passed through them, districts that melt into one another without climax." In the same way that Bishop Berkeley's God has to be in the forest when nobody else is, to hear the tree falling, the raven allows Fisher to assert an imaginative claim to parts of his city he hasn't ever bothered to visit. Unlike Yeats's fantastic bird singing for the lords and ladies of Byzantium, the albino raven is the work of puffy-eyed and crablike artisans who supply pet-shops or garden centres. Amid such multiple resignations of the Romantic inheritance does Fisher reign over the peculiar domain of *The Cut Pages*, with a mixture of implacability and bewilderment: "Slowly this bird and I are working on each other. The only rule in our game is that neither of us must appear to change." "So hoarily embedded in symbolism" in appearance, it can only be bad manners on the bird's part not to croak an obliging "Nevermore" from time to time. But no, it won't. As Fisher writes of another bird, the "great fat thrush" of the book's last section, 'The Flight Orator', "He may be dead; he may be struggling under the ground for a long while. Nothing can reach him. Nothing of this will ever be repeated." Any further inquiries can to referred to the final *Watt* addendum: "no symbols where none intended". And yet the effect of all this atomisation and flux is not to silence Fisher's work; its singular achievement is, patiently, ingeniously, to make these very things speak. As he writes at the end of 'Toyland' of his T.F. Powys-like townsfolk going about their business:

> The secret laugh of the world picks them up and shakes them
>   like peas boiling;
> They behave as if nothing happened; maybe they no longer
>   notice.

the fisher syndrome explained

> I notice. I laugh with the laugh, cultivate it, make much of it,
> But still I don't know what the joke is, to tell them.

Fisher's poetry picks its readers up and gives them a good shake, but only the most obtuse could behave as if nothing were happening. Most will have the good sense to acknowledge how they have been marked with a permanent but indefinable response, at once subtle and momentous, a mixture of a smirk and a grimace at the secret laugh of the world.

2

In a gloriously silly Monty Python sketch, a Hungarian enters an English tobacconist's and with the help of an unreliable phrasebook attempts to buy some cigarettes and matches. His outpourings range from "My hovercraft is full of eels" and "'I will not buy this record, it is scratched", to "Do you want to come back to my place, bouncy bouncy?" He doesn't get very far, and before long the publisher of the phrasebook is being put on trial for breach of the peace. It's an example that anyone trying to write a reader's guide to the strange dialect that is contemporary British poetry would do well to bear in mind. The spectre of befuddlement is never far away: just ask American readers asked to choose between Keith Tuma's *Fishing by Obstinate Isles* (1998) and Dana Gioia's *Barrier of a Common Language* (2003) as accurate translations of the state of British poetry now. It does not take the Atlantic for barriers to go up: Gioia's title might as well be a reference to the gulf between his canon and Tuma's. Where the latter's bouncy-bouncy roadmap reads Mina Loy, Tom Raworth and Lee Harwood, Gioia's hovercraft travels by way of James Fenton, Charles Causley and Philip Larkin. Just occasionally, though, there are overlaps. Both men share an interest in Charles Tomlinson and Donald Davie, poets whose pedigree and profile defy simple categorisation. To continue the roadmap metaphor, a reader standing on Tomlinson-Davie Avenue can choose to proceed in a number of directions. If that reader is Gioia, he will head on back to the Hughes-Larkin metropolis, and if he is Tuma he will strike out for the less charted territories of Christopher Middleton and the subject of this review, Roy Fisher. For the great majority of American readers who are not Keith Tuma, though, it can't be said often enough: Fisherville is a part of town you've got to visit, now.

As anyone familiar with his very funny poem 'On the Neglect of Figure Composition' will know, Roy Fisher needs no lessons in Monty Python-style absurdism. After all, any attempt to sketch the vagaries of his reputation involves large doses of it. As a beginner, he succeeded in acquiring an American reputation almost before he acquired a British one. It's a tale Fisher has often told in interview (Fisher gives a very good interview: cf. *Interviews Through Time and Selected Prose* [Shearsman Books, 2000]), but having published his important early work *City* in 1961 to minimal response at home, he found a much more receptive welcome in journals such as Cid Corman's *Origin* and other "Black Mountain spin-off publications". It helped that, in Britain, he was published by the enterprising Fulcrum Press, whose other authors included Ed Dorn, Lorine Niedecker and Robert Duncan: bracing company for an English poet to be keeping, in those post-ration book days. Yet ask an American reader today for the name of a mid- to late-century British poet and the answer, if not Ted Hughes, will be Larkin. Why?

Because it didn't come off, that's why. The Fulcrum connection opened American doors for Fisher, but if he didn't catch on it's because the moment of radical promise represented by Fulcrum didn't last, and neither did the left-field "British Poetry Revival" associated with it. In a kind of *Paradise Lost* narrative involving a treacherous Arts Council and the sacking of editor Eric Mottram from *Poetry Review*, the helots did down the zealots, and the radical energies of British poetry were driven underground, where (the story goes) they have mostly remained to this day. While Fisher has published with moderate to large publishing houses in the years that followed (Oxford, Carcanet, and now Bloodaxe), he has enjoyed neither the anointed radical status of Creeley or Olson in the States, the cult of (anti-)personality associated with the British radical school's exhibit-in-chief, J.H. Prynne, or, needless to say, the popular success of his more broadsheet-friendly British contemporaries. He has been, in his inspirational way, a kind of nowhere man of British poetry for the last fifty years, hugely deserving of the popular readership he has neither courted nor showily disdained. He has simply done his own thing. And when it comes to *The Long and the Short of It*, he's done

the fisher syndrome explained

---

it again: if you're a reader who likes to get a chronological sense of what happened when, and where all these individual poems come from, this book will provoke your instant wrath. Fisher has lumped all his poems in together in an a-historical sequence of his own choosing; the fact that the index at the back lists some poems as dating from the year '0000' seems oddly appropriate.

It takes until line three of the first poem here, 'Wonders of Obligation', before we get our first mention of brickwork, a theme that assumes almost King Charles' Head-like proportions in Fisher's work. A typical Fisher poem will be set in Birmingham, the West Midlands or the Pennines, preferably with some post-industrial factory fronts to hand and a late bus trundling past, and the slowly clenching fist of evening squeezing the light out of the scene, leaving its dancing forms on the brickwork as it goes. So much stone and shadow may not look like they've got much to say for themselves, but as Fisher writes at the end of 'The Dow Low Drop':

> Not only in desert cliffs,
> rock-fares of affront,
> cities of single rooms
> piled along ravines,
>
> but from afternoon shadows
> and the crevices of seats by night
> there's a wonderful
> growl to be heard.

Pronouns will be elusive and unsatisfactory: a straightforwardly first-person lyric such as 'The Entertainment of War' (from *City*), fine poem though it is, is one you can bet gets on its author's nerves, and you'd be right. There is the opposite temptation too, of outright syntactic apocalypse, as explored in *The Cut Pages* at the end of the 60s, but not enforced in the books that followed. He was feeling a bit depressed at the time, as he likes to explain. Welfare State Britain may seem ubiquitous, as illustrated by Raymond Briggs, all drainpipes and compost heaps, yet altogether more unruly spirits are at large, such as John Cowper Powys, whose ley lines run through the middle of the great long poem

David Wheatley

A Furnace, doing his best for the desired ambience of "polytheism without gods." The soundtrack will be the kind of jazz Fisher has played all his life on the piano, and which provides the key signature to 'The Thing About Joe Sullivan', "jamming sound against idea //hard as it can go /florid and dangerous." The grotesque will occasionally obtrude, as in that "foetus in the dustbin mov[ing] one claw" in *City*, but the tone will more usually tend towards dryness and self-distancing. This is writing in which "the nondescript /silently fights for its life", "what's now only disproved /was once imagined", containing "above all /no 'atmosphere'", that "doesn't aim to please /and for the most part doesn't", hymning "the ghost of a paper bag", and like a Movement refusenik aspiring only to the "well made crisis."

Only another Monty Python reference, the Summarize Proust Competition this time, can lend any dignity to my attempts to convey the full range of this book in a mere review, but its nine sub-sections are roughly as follows. One: main courses first, with only 'Wonders of Obligation' and 'The Dow Low Drop' to soften us up before *City, A Furnace, The Cut Pages* and *The Ship's Orchestra* one after the other. Two: a crepuscular interlude, a drawing of breath, a small Pennine village barely more than its welcome sign. Three: literary pasquinades, including 'On the Neglect of Figure Composition' and Fisher's correspondence with Ms Avis Tree in 'Paraphrases', and the star-crossed pair's attempts to set up a flying rendezvous on Rugby railway station platform ("the train / goes through without stopping"). Four: more railways and allegorical pieces ('Toyland'), the odd attempt, quickly defused, at what sounds like a statement of first principles ('The Open Poem and the Closed Poem'). Five: homages, to Edwin Morgan, Gael Turnbull, Geoffrey Hill and others. Six: workshop pieces, declarations of intent and mini-manifestoes such as 'It is Writing' ("I mistrust the poem in the hour of its success.") Seven: the hypnotic claustrophobia of 'Interiors with Various Figures', the chthonic cinema of 'Handsworth Liberties', and then some real 'Texts for a Film' (from *Birmingham River*). Eight: epigraphs and graffiti, and the borderline Peter Reading routines of 'Figures from Anansi Company' ("Ouf. Ouf. Ouf. Ouf. Ouf" goes 'Dog.') And nine: a slight nip in the air, between 'Why They Stopped Singing', 'Last Poems' and 'As He Came Near Death' ("After a time the grave got up and went away.") And that's it. Among

the fisher syndrome explained

---

the new poems scattered through the book (neophytes will need that date-lined index to work out which they are), I like 'Mother-Tongue, Father-Tongue', with its schmaltz-free raid on Tony Harrison territory: "*Summat o' that. Ah*", says the ghostly parental voice, "Meaning yes. // *Ah.*"

I can't think of an English poet today whose work has given me more pleasure. Readers yet to tune their ears to the endlessly subtle harmonies and pleasures of his work would be well advised to get cracking on *The Long and the Short of It: Poems 1955–2005* as their all-in-one Roy Fisher phrasebook. Only one curse will suffice for those unadventurous souls who refuse: may your hovercraft be full of eels!

a bibliography

DEREK SLADE

The More He Looked

"The more he looked / the more he saw." So says Roy Fisher in the fifth of 'The Six Deliberate Acts.' This has certainly been my experience in compiling a bibliography of works by and about Roy, initially for private publication in 1987, then in extended form for *The Thing about Roy Fisher* (2000) and now covering the years 2000–2010 (overleaf). I'd begun reading Roy's work in the early 1970s, alerted to its existence by two Penguin anthologies: Edward Lucie-Smith's *British Poetry since 1945* and Jon Silkin's *Poetry of the Committed Individual*. (Both books, in their various ways, displaying an eclecticism that still seems admirable, and only matched recently by Keith Tuma and Nate Dorward's *Anthology of British & Irish Poetry*.) What struck me about Roy's poems in these books was, quite simply, how different they were than the poetry I'd been thinking of as contemporary—I'd survived two degrees in English with the belief that Faber & Faber had modern poetry pretty well sewn up. Here was someone who occasionally used rhyme and, to bend slightly one of Roy's statements, could commit the odd iambic pentameter, but who was also using forms I just hadn't come across before (notably the use of indented lines in 'Seven Attempted Moves' and the verse-paragraphs in 'Interior 1') and, equally important, writing about things not entirely foreign to my own experience. Born and brought up over a hundred miles south of Birmingham, I'd nevertheless seen "gardens / Small enough for pets' droppings / quickly to cover" and "dirt / Stained through with oils", though I hadn't seen poets who had thought to write about these. I could also see from the anthologies that Roy wasn't just down and dirty, of course, and when I had the good fortune to pick up a copy of the Fulcrum *Collected Poems* I realised that this was a poetry I would want to keep re-reading and to keep up with. So I began looking for what else Roy had written and done, and for what others had made of his work. By the summer of 1985 ("the dog days?" Roy once enquired) it occurred to me that the mass of books, pamphlets, magazines, clippings and other material I'd acquired might be shaped into a form useful for other readers of Roy's work. This also meant that I'd have to look harder for what I'd missed.

As I looked, what did I see? Above all, I saw the extraordinary range of Roy Fisher's career. I found poems published in the most fugitive of little mags, and also in *Palgrave's Golden Treasury*. I found that he has been translated into Romanian, French, Spanish, Italian and Russian, and done translations himself of the Russian poet Mariya Kildibekova and also of texts for Schubert song-cycles, subsequently recorded by Shura Gehrman and released on CD. His recorded readings have been made available as an LP album, cassettes, CDs and most recently in digital format on the Archive of the Now website. His collaborations with artists include a relatively modestly produced poster poem with David Prentice but also hugely expensive joint works with Ron King for Circle Press. He has been the subject of six-line reviews and of PhD theses. There have been over fifteen published interviews and an *Antebiography*, which is both remarkably frank about his early years and his starting points as a poet and which also provides a fascinating social history view of Handsworth. He has made many radio broadcasts including a programme where he shared a studio with Rabbi Lionel Blue, and he has appeared as the subject of a film by Tom Pickard. For someone occasionally described as self-effacing, this is not bad going. And while Roy once, in an interview with Eric Mottram, characterised his career as "enormously passive", what I see, finally, is a body of work whose extent perhaps surprises Roy himself.

a bibliography

Roy Fisher: A Bibliography 2000–2010

Most of the following items appeared after the publication of *The Thing About Roy Fisher* (Liverpool University Press, 2000), though some are earlier ones I missed when compiling the bibliography printed in that book. Section headings correspond to those in the Liverpool book, except for the last two, which are new.

A. BOOKS AND PAMPHLETS BY ROY FISHER

[*Twentieth Century English Poetry*, CD-ROM published by Chadwyck-Healey, contains the full texts of *CP55–87*, *The Cut Pages*, *DLD* and *BR*. Cambridge, 2001.]

The Long and the Short of It: Poems 1955–2005, Newcastle upon Tyne, Bloodaxe, 2005 [hereafter *LSI*]

Standard Midland, Newcastle upon Tyne, Bloodaxe, 2010. Contents: 'The After-life', 'On Spare Land', 'Somewhere along the Pool', 'Inner Voice', 'On the Wellingtonias at Pilleth', 'On Hearing I'd Outlived My Son the Linguist', 'Little Jazz', 'Target', 'Jumping the Gun', 'Impurities', 'False Winds', 'Sanctuary', 'Syntax', 'Plot', 'A Damp Night', 'The Skyline in the Wall Mirror', 'Dancing Neanderthal', 'At Brough-on-Noe', 'Adjectives: the Novel, the Movie', 'Shocking Pink', 'Long Ago in a Town in the Provinces', 'Travel', 'Log', 'Of the Qualities', 'Hole Horse and Hellbox', 'Peeling', 'A Masque of Resistances', 'The Run to Brough', 'Stops and Stations', 'Rattle a Cart'.

An Unofficial Roy Fisher, ed. Peter Robinson. Exeter, Shearsman Books, 2010. This includes the following mostly uncollected poems by RF: 'A Vision of Four Musicians', 'The Doctor Died', 'Double Morning', 'Heroic Landscape', 'Divisions', 'Night Walkers', 'Script City', 'Something Unmade', 'Results', 'Last Brief Maxims', 'After Midnight', 'The Bachelors Stripped Bare by Their Bride', 'Division of Labour', 'Uncle Jim's Will', 'Big Girl', 'The Discovery of Metre', 'Abraham Darby's Bridge', '"Dear Gael"', '"Neighbours, We'll Not Part Tonight"', 'Art Comes to its Senses Again', 'A Poetry List'.

Selected Poems, Chicago, Flood Editions. Scheduled for publication late 2010–early 2011. Edited and with a Foreword by August Kleinzahler. Provisional list of contents: from *City* ('City', 'The Entertainment of War', 'The Sun Hacks', 'The Poplars', 'Starting to Make a Tree', "I Want to Believe…"), 'Linear', from *The Ship's Orchestra,* from *Interiors with Various Figures* ('The Steam Crane', 'The Wrestler', 'The Foyer', 'The Billiard Table'), 'After Working', 'The Thing About Joe Sullivan', 'For Realism', 'The Memorial Fountain', 'Metamorphoses', 'One World', '107 Poems', 'In the Wall', 'It Is Writing', 'The Only Image', 'Of the Empirical Self and for Me', 'If I Didn't', 'Style', 'Discovering the Form', 'Wonders of Obligation', 'The Open Poem and the Closed Poem', 'The Home Pianist's Companion', 'Provision', 'The Running Changes', 'The Lesson in Composition', from *A Furnace* ('Colossus'), 'Going', 'Freelance', 'A Working Devil for the Birthday of Coleman Hawkins', 'The Slink', 'Item', 'At the Grave of Asa Benveniste', 'The Dow Low Drop', 'And on That Note: Six Jazz Elegies', 'False Winds', 'Inner Voice', 'Little Jazz', 'Syntax', 'On the Wellingtonias at Pilleth', 'The Afterlife', 'Rattle a Cart'.

B. Collaborations with Artists

Tabernacle. Hole, horse & hell-box, London, Circle Press, 2001. A cabinet containing 6 cases. Case 1, *hole*, is a bound book with verse by RF and graphics by Ronald King. An edition of 56 signed copies.

Cooking the Books: Ron King and Circle Press, Andrew Lambirth (essay), Ron King (descriptions and commentary), New Haven, Connecticut, Yale Centre for British Art; and London, Circle Press, 2002. References to RF on pp. 14, 62, 64, 68, 82, 87, 90, 95, 146. Colour images of collaborations between RF and Ron King: 'Bluebeard's Castle' (pp.45–49), '"Neighbours We'll Not Part Tonight"' (pp.54–55), 'Scenes from the Alphabet' (p.69), 'The Half-Year Letters' (p.100), 'The Left-Handed Punch' (pp.106–111), 'Anansi Company' (pp.127–133), 'Roller' (p.154), 'Tabernacle' (pp.155–161). Reproduction of 'E' from 'The Half-Year Letters' inset between pages 64 and 65. See Section D below for details of an interview with RF contained in this book.

a bibliography

C. Composition Chronology and details of publication

1957
'Why They Stopped Singing'
    La isla tuerta: 49 poetas británicos, 1946–2006, ed. and translated into Spanish by Matías Serra Bradford, Barcelona, Lumen, 2009.

'Toyland'
    New Penguin Book of English Verse, ed. Paul Keegan. Harmondsworth, Penguin Books, 2000

1960 (*City*)
'The Entertainment of War'
    Not to Speak of the Dog: 101 Short Stories in Verse, ed. Christopher Reid, London, Faber & Faber, 2000

    Anthology of Twentieth-Century British and Irish Poetry, ed. Keith Tuma, New York, Oxford University Press, 2001

'By the Pond'
    New Penguin Book of English Verse

'Starting to Make a Tree'
    Red Sky at Night: An Anthology of British Socialist Poetry, Eds. Andy Croft and Adrian Mitchell, Nottingham, Five Leaves Publications, 2003

'The Poplars'
    Anthology of Twentieth-Century British and Irish Poetry

Prose-section beginning 'Walking through the suburb…'
    Anthology of Twentieth-Century British and Irish Poetry

    Here to Eternity: An Anthology of Poetry, ed. Andrew Motion, London, Faber & Faber, 2001

'As He Came Near Death'
    New Penguin Book of English Verse

1965
'The Thing about Joe Sullivan'
Paging Doctor Jazz: a Verse Anthology,
ed. John Lucas, Nottingham, Shoestring Press, 2004

La isla tuerta: 49 poetas británicos, 1946–2006.
English text, and translation into Spanish by the editor

'The Memorial Fountain'
New Penguin Book of English Verse

'From an English Sensibility'
Anthology of Twentieth-Century British and Irish Poetry

'For Realism'
The North, 35, 2004,
ed. Peter Sansom and Janet Fisher, Huddersfield

1967
'The Making of the Book'
La isla tuerta: 49 poetas británicos, 1946–2006.
English text, and translation into Spanish by the editor

1970
'The Cut Pages'
Passages in *Vanishing Points*, ed. Rod Mengham and John Kinsella, Cambridge and Applecross, Western Australia, Salt Publishing, 2004

1975
'Dusk'
Poem for the Day: Two, ed. R.Bowen, N. Temple, S.Wienrich, N. Albery, London, Chatto and Windus, 2003

1977
'Style'
La isla tuerta: 49 poetas británicos, 1946–2006.
English text, and translation into Spanish by the editor

1980
'The Home Pianist's Companion'
Paging Doctor Jazz: a Verse Anthology

1981
'The Running Changes'
An Accessible Paradise, Carlisle, East Cumbria Countryside Project, 2007

1982
'Masterpieces in My Sleep'
La isla tuerta: 49 poetas británicos, 1946–2006. English text, and translation into Spanish by the editor

1983
From *A Furnace*: 'Entroit' and 'The Return'
Anthology of Twentieth-Century British and Irish Poetry

1985
'The Nation'
Staying Alive: Real Poems for Unreal Times, ed. Neil Astley, Tarset, Bloodaxe, 2002

'They Come Home'
Contemporary Poetry: Poets and Poetry since 1990, Ian Brinton. Cambridge, Cambridge University Press, 2009

'The Toy'
La isla tuerta: 49 poetas británicos, 1946–2006. English text, and translation into Spanish by the editor

1988
'Going'
Contemporary Poetry: Poets and Poetry since 1990

1990
'The Host'
Time's Tidings: Greeting the 21st Century, ed. Carol Ann Duffy, London, Anvil Press Poetry, 1999

1991
'Abstracted Water'
The River's Voice, ed. Angela King and Susan Clifford, Dorset, Green Books, 2001

'Birmingham River'
The River's Voice

1992
'Photographers' Flowers'
La isla tuerta: 49 poetas británicos, 1946–2006. English text, and translation into Spanish by the editor

'For Ian Tyson at 60'
Terrible Work, 2, Autumn 1993, ed. Tim Allen, Plymouth

1993
'Bing-bong Ladies from Tongue Lane'
Terrible Work, 2, Autumn 1993

1994
'And on that Note: Jazz Elegies'
Notre Dame Review, 11, Winter 2001, ed. John Matthias and William O'Rourke, Indiana

Paging Doctor Jazz: a Verse Anthology

1996
'At the Grave of Asa Benveniste'
La isla tuerta: 49 poetas británicos, 1946–2006. English text, and translation into Spanish by the editor

a bibliography

1999
'Processional: For Lee Harwood'
　Notre Dame Review, 11, Winter 2001

'Night Sees Day' (21 February 1999)
　Oasis, 100, June 2000, ed. Ian Robinson, London

'Noted' (24–28 August 1999)
　Oasis, 100, June 2000

'Custom' (27–28 August 1999)
　Oasis, 100, June 2000

2000
'Routine Check' (14 February 2000)
　Poems for the Waiting Room, a pack of specially commissioned poems, distributed by Hyphen-21, Cardiff, 2000

'You Should Have Been There' (30 March 2000)
　April Eye: Poems for Peter Riley, ed. Peter Hughes. Cambridge, Infernal Methods, 2000

　Notre Dame Review, 11, Winter 2001

'*From* The Dow Low Drop' (6–28 August 2000)
　Notre Dame Review, 11, Winter 2001
　(These are different passages than those published in *DLD*.)

2004
'The Badger's Belly-mark' (November 2002)
　Raw Edge, 19, Autumn–Winter, 2004–5,
　ed. Dave Reeves, Birmingham.

'Mother-tongue, Father-tongue' (27 August 2004)
　Raw Edge, 19, Autumn–Winter, 2004–5

2005
'Homilies' (2 October 2004)
   SENTENCE: a journal of prose poetics (special feature on British prose poetry, edited & introduced by N. Santilli) 3, 2005

2007
'Announcement' (29 October 2002)
   Stand, 182 (7:2), 2007

'Inner Voice' (10 October 2006)
   Stand, 182 (7:2), 2007

'On Spare Land' (6 October 2006)
   Stand, 182 (7:2), 2007

'Syntax' (7 August 1999)
   Stand, 182 (7:2), 2007

'The Afterlife' (4 February 2006)
   Stand, 182 (7:2), 2007

'Travel' (10 October 2006)
   Stand, 182 (7:2), 2007

'A Mellstock Fiddle' (26 July 2006)
   Answering Back, ed. Carol Ann Duffy. London, Picador, 2007 (Written as a response to Thomas Hardy's 'She Saw Him, She Said'.)

D. INTERVIEWS WITH ROY FISHER

The Inky, 15, Sheffield, June/July/August 2000, unpaginated. The interviewer is Dave Sissons.

Cooking the Books: Ron King and Circle Press, Andrew Lambirth (essay), Ron King (descriptions and commentary), New Haven, Connecticut,

a bibliography

Yale Centre for British Art; and London, Circle Press, 2002. 'An Epistolary Dialogue with Roy Fisher', pp. 141–146. The interviewer is Andrew Lambirth.

City Life, 479, Manchester, April 2003, p.26. Ra Page, 'Cry Me a River'.

'Come to think of it, the imagination.' Interview with John Kerrigan. First published in *News for the Ear: A Homage to Roy Fisher* (Exeter: Stride Publications, 2000), this interview is now available in the on-line magazine, Jacket, at http://jacketmagazine.com/35/iv-fisher-ivb-kerrigan.shtml

E. Critical and other Prose by Roy Fisher

The Star You Steer By: Basil Bunting and British Modernism, ed. James McGonical and Richard Price. Amsterdam/Atlanta GA, Rodopi, 2001. 'Debt to Mr Bunting', pp.11–16.

Poet's Poems 6, series edited by Stuart Mills. Derbyshire, Aggie Weston's Editions, 2001. RF provides a brief (two-sentence) postscript on his choice of poems. Unpaginated.

Jacket 22, May 2003. Available at http://jacketmagazine.com/22/caddel.html 'Prose memoir' [of Richard Caddel].

Selected Poems by Jeff Nuttall. Cambridge, Salt Publishing, 2004. Introduction, p.xvii.

Spleen, Nicholas Moore. Foreword by RF. An on-line version is available at http://www.ubu.com/ubu/pdf/moore_spleen.pdf

There are words: Collected Poems, Gael Turnbull. Exeter, Shearsman Books, 2006. Back cover contains a tribute to Gael Turnbull by RF.

Starting at Zero, ed. Nicholas Johnson. Exbourne, Etruscan Books, 2007. Contains 'At A Tangent', a brief account of RF's responses to the Black Mountain poets.

The Salt Companion to Peter Robinson, ed. Adam Piette and Katy Price. Cambridge, Salt, 2007. Preface by RF, pp.21–25. See also the

Introduction, pp. 5, 15 for references to RF.

Down to Earth, John Wilkinson. Cambridge, Salt, 2008. Commendatory sentence by RF. The sentence is taken from the interview with John Kerrigan published in *News for the Ear: A Homage to Roy Fisher* and also available on-line as part of *Jacket* magazine (see Section D above).

The Powys Journal, Vol. 18, 2008. 'On JCP's Letters (with two letters from JCP to Fisher)', pp. 30–37. RF discusses his brief correspondence with John Cowper Powys.

Uplift: A Samizdat for Lee Harwood from his Friends, ed. Patricia Hope Scanlan. Hove, Artery Editions, 2008. 'My Trip to Brighton', p. 10.

An Unofficial Roy Fisher, ed. Peter Robinson. Exeter, Shearsman Books, 2010. 'Death by Adjectives'.

F. Radio broadcasts and recorded readings

(2) Recorded readings

Roy Fisher. A CD, produced by The Poetry Archive, Gloucestershire, 2004. Recorded on September 25, 2002. RF reads 'At the Grave of Asa Benveniste', 'The House on the Border'. 'Near Garmsley Camp', '3rd November 1976', 'They Come Home', 'Hynopaedia', 'Top Down, Bottom Up', 'Abstracted Water', 'Birmingham River', 'The Host', 'Promenade On Down', 'The Collection of Things', 'The Lesson in Composition', 'Butterton Ford', 'The Burning Graves at Netherton', 'Matrix', 'The Six Deliberate Acts', 'Three Ceremonial Poems', 'Handsworth Liberties', 'Staffordshire Red', 'The Trace', 'The Sidings at Drebkau', 'Discovering the Form', 'You Should Have Been There', 'Processional', 'Noted'.

Archive of the Now: this on-line repository of readings and textual material contains a reading by RF of 'A Furnace' (section 2), 'Homilies', 'Processional', 'Songs from the Camel's Coffin', 'The Memorial Fountain', 'The Red and the Black', 'The Trace', 'You Should Have Been There.' Recorded on September 3, 2005. Available at http://www.archiveofthenow.com/

a bibliography

The British Library Sound Archive contains an extensive collection (currently 178 items) of recordings of RF, including poetry readings, radio talks and discussions, and piano-playing. The Sound Archive catalogue can be accessed at http://cadensa.bl.uk/cgi-bin/webcat

G. ON ROY FISHER

Orizont, 2, 1974. (Timisoara, Romania). Dumitru Ciociopop: translations of, and commentaries on, poems by RF.

Albion, 13, 1981 (published by Appalachian State University, North Carolina). Janet L. Somerville: 'Roy Fisher's Poetry of Freeplay".

Yearbook of English Studies, 17, 1987. John Lucas: 'English Poets and American Jazz'. Commentary on 'The Thing about Joe Sullivan', pp.59–61.

Agenda, 29:4, 1991. Kenneth Cox, 'Roy Fisher', pp.31–40.

Bloomsbury Guides to English Literature: The Twentieth Century, ed. Linda R. Williams, London, Bloomsbury, 1992. p.105. Contains a brief biographical and bibliographical account.

Eric Mottram Archive, King's College London. Contains materials from and relating to RF. Catalogue available at http://www.kcl.ac.uk/depsta/iss/archives/collect/1mo70-05a.html

'Entrancements on the local bus': review of DLD by Jeff Nuttall. *The Independent*, 02.03.96.

Prose Studies 20:1, 1997. Nikki Santilli, 'The Prose Poem and the City', pp. 77–89.

Orbis, 116/117, Spring 2000, pp.91–93. 'Lives and Letters': review by Alexis Lykiard of *ITT*.

The Thing About Roy Fisher: Critical Studies, ed. John Kerrigan and Peter Robinson. Liverpool, Liverpool University Press, 2000.

PQR, 16, Spring 2000, pp.6–7. Review by Peter Riley of *ITT*.

Yale Journal of Criticism, 13:1, Spring 2000, pp.87–106. Peter Barry, '"Birmingham's What I Think With": Roy Fisher's Composite Epic'. In the same issue: pp.107–128. Clive Bush, 'In Sight and Time: Some Patterns of Appearance in Roy Fisher's Poetry'.

Contemporary British Poetry and the City, Peter Barry. Manchester, Manchester University Press, 2000. Chapter 8, pp. 193–222. '"Birmingham's What I Think With": Roy Fisher's Cities'. A version of the Peter Barry article in *Yale Journal of Criticism*, 13:1 (see above).

Terrible Work, 10, Summer 2000, p.78. Review by Oliver Ahearn of *ITT*.

Jacket, 12, July 2000. Review by Nate Dorward of *ITT*, *NE* and *The Thing About Roy Fisher*. This on-line review is available at http://jacketmagazine.com/jacket12/fisher-by-dorward.html.

PN Review, 136, 27:2, 2000, pp.57-58. Review by William Wootten of *The Thing About Roy Fisher*. Available on-line at: http://www.pnreview.co.uk/cgi-bin/scribe?file=/members/pnr136/reviews/136rv04.txt.

Who's Who in Twentieth Century World Poetry. Ed. Mark Willhardt, London and New York, Routledge, 2000, p.170. Brief biographical and bibliographical account.

Raw Edge, 11, Autumn/Winter 2000, p.27. Review by David Hart of *ITT* and *NE*.

Acumen, 39, January 2001, pp.119–122. 'Barnadine's Reply': review by John Goodby of *ITT*.

Poetry Review, 9:4, Winter 2000/1, pp.67–70. 'Barnadine's Reply': review by John Goodby of *The Thing About Roy Fisher* and *NE*.

Notre Dame Review, 11, Winter 2001, pp.173–179. 'Maps to Roy Fisher': review by Devin Johnston of *ITT*, *NE* and *The Thing About Roy Fisher*.

Anthology of Twentieth-Century British and Irish Poetry, ed. Keith Tuma. New York and Oxford, Oxford University Press, 2001, pp.537–538. Brief critical account by the editor.

a bibliography

The North, 28, 2001, p.48. Review by Steven Waling of *ITT*.

Collected Studies in the Use of English, Kenneth Cox. London, Agenda Editions, 2001, pp.84–96. 'Roy Fisher'. (Originally published in *Agenda*, 29:4, 1991, see above.)

10th Muse, 11, 2001, p.54. Review by Andrew Jordan of *ITT*. This review is available on-line at http://www.poetrymagazines.org.uk/magazine/record.asp?id=15705

Cambridge Quarterly, 30:2, 2001, pp. 175–179. 'Poetry and Pragmatism: New Things about Roy Fisher': review by Raphael Ingelbein of *ITT, NE* and *The Thing About Roy Fisher*.

Thumbscrew, 19, Autumn 2001, pp.41–44. 'De-anglicising England': review by Arthur Aughey of *ITT, NE* and *The Thing About Roy Fisher*.

PQR, 18, 2002, p.9. 'Beyond Modesty': review by Keith Jebb of *ITT* and *NE*.

Review of English Studies, 53:3, 2002, pp.466–467. Review by Stan Smith of *The Thing About Roy Fisher*.

English, 51, Summer 2002, pp.185–192. 'The Editorial Commentary' by Peter Barry contains an extended commentary on *The Thing About Roy Fisher*.

The Modern Language Review 97:2, 2002, pp.409–410. Review by J. Cowley of *The Thing About Roy Fisher, ITT and News for the Ear*. This review is available on-line at http://findarticles.com/p/articles/mi_7026/is_2_97/ai_n28130500/pg_1.

Such Rare Citings: the prose poem in English literature, Nikki Santilli. Madison: Fairleigh Dickinson University Press and New Jersey: Associated University Presses, 2002.

The Continuum Encyclopaedia of British Literature, ed. Steven R. Serafin and Valerie Grosvenor Myer. New York and London, Continuum, 2002. Contains an entry on RF by David Fulton.

The Failure of Conservatism in Modern British Poetry, Andrew Duncan.

Cambridge and Applecross, Western Australia, Salt Publishing, 2003. References to RF on pp. 12,18, 34, 43, 47, 75–76, 96, 98-99, 171–173, 175, 204, 229, 252, 283, 316, 340.

Poetry Ireland Review, 77, Autumn 2003, pp.40–47. David Wheatley, '"Exposed to the Open at All Events": On Roy Fisher's *The Cut Pages*'.

The North, 35, 2004, pp. 18–19. Responses to 'For Realism' (printed without RF's name, as a blind criticism exercise).

Cercles, 12, 2005, pp.79–93. William Wootten, 'Romanticism and Animism in Roy Fisher's *A Furnace*'. This essay is available on-line at www.cercles.com/n12/wootten.pdf

Stride Magazine, 2005. Martin Caseley, 'Thinking with Birmingham': a review of *LSI*. This review is available on-line at: http://www.stridemagazine.co.uk/, in the archive section.

The Poetry of Saying: British Poetry and its Discontents, Robert Sheppard. Liverpool, University of Liverpool Press, 2005. Chapter Three: 'Starting to Make a World: The Poetry of Roy Fisher.' Other references to RF *passim*.

Twentieth Century Poetry: Selves and Situations, Peter Robinson. Oxford, Oxford University Press, 2005. Chapter 12: 'Roy Fisher's Last Things.' This essay originally appeared in *The Thing About Roy Fisher*.

'The Measure of the Muse': review of *LSI* by William Wootten. *Guardian*, 29.10.05, Review section (p.18). This review is available on-line at: http://www.guardian.co.uk/books/2005/oct/29/featuresreviews.guardianreview34

'Christmas Books Special: Poetry reviewed': includes brief review of LSI by Michael Glover. *The Independent*, 02.12.05.

'A maestro who moves to the beat of the American avant-garde': review of *LSI* by William Palmer. *The Independent*, 28.12.05.

The North, 37, 2005, pp.17–31. Paul Mills, 'Action and Inertia: Ted Hughes and Roy Fisher.' Includes review of *LSI*.

Orbis, 135, Winter 2005, pp.42–44. 'A Life's Work': review of *LSI* by Andy Brown.

a bibliography

Dictionary of Literary Biography [2005–06]. An essay on RF by Deborah Mitchell. This essay is available at http://www.bookrags.com/biography/roy-fisher-dlb/ A subscription is required to access the full essay.

'Britain, their Britain': includes review of *LSI* by Sean O'Brien. *The Sunday Times*, 01.01.06.

PN Review, 168 (32:4), March–April 2006, pp. 59–60. 'All said and done': review of *LSI* by Matthew Sperling. On-line at: http://www.pnreview.co.uk/cgi-bin/scribe?file=/members/pnr168/reviews/168rv06.txt

London Review of Books: 28:8, 20 April 2006. 'Snarly Glitters': review by August Kleinzahler of *LSI*. This review is also available on-line at http://www.lrb.co.uk/v28/n08/klei01_.html.

Poetry Nottingham: 60:1, Spring 2006. Review by Alan Baker of *LSI*. This review is also available on-line at http://www.leafepress.com/litter1/baker02/fisher%20review.html as part of *Litter* e-zine.

Agenda: 42:1, 2006, pp.42–46. 'Landscapes and Traditions': review by Martin Dodsworth of *LSI*.

Poetry Wars, Peter Barry. Cambridge, Salt Publishing, 2006. Although he is not listed in the index, references to RF occur on pp. xiv, 45–46, 66, 81, 94, 114, 117, 118, 119, 211, 212, 220.

Notre Dame Review: 22, Summer 2006. 'Keeping it Strange': review by Peter Robinson of *LSI*. This review is available online at http://www.nd.edu/~ndr/issues/ndr22/Peter%20Robinson/Robinson-review.pdf

Shearsman: 69 & 70, Autumn 2006/Winter 2007, pp.94–101. 'The Later Fisher': essay by Peter Makin.

Poetry Ireland Review, 88, December 2006, pp.72–75. 'A Hovercraft Full of Eels': review by David Wheatley of *LSI*.

The London Magazine, December 2006/January 2007, pp.104–108. 'The Sun is Written On': review by Sean Elliott of *LSI*.

Stand, 182 (7:2), 2007, pp.61–68. 'Art's Marvellous': review by Jeffrey Wainwright of *LSI*.

PN Review, 174 (33:4), March–April 2007, pp.29–33. Richard Price, 'Migrant the Magnificent.' References to RF throughout. Available on-line at: http://www.pnreview.co.uk/cgi-bin/scribe?file=/members/pnr174/articles/174ar02.txt

On Form: Poetry, Aestheticism and the Legacy of a Word, Angela Leighton. Oxford, Oxford University Press, 2007. Chapter 10: 'Forms of Elegy: Stevenson, Muldoon, Hill, Fisher.' Other references to RF on pp. 264, 271, 277, 279, 281.

The All-Sustaining Air: Romantic Legacies and Renewals in British, American and Irish Poetry since 1900, Michael O'Neill. Oxford, Oxford University Press, 2007. Chapter 8: '"Deep Shocks of Recognition" and "Gutted" Romanticism: Geoffrey Hill and Roy Fisher.'

'"The Making of the Book": Roy Fisher, the Circle Press and the Poetics of Book Art', Matthew Sperling, *Literature Compass* 4 (2007). A subscription to *Literature Compass* (an on-line scholarly journal) is required to access the full essay. Go to: http://www.blackwell-compass.com/subject/literature/

The Oxford Handbook of British and Irish War Poetry, ed. Tim Kendall. Oxford, Oxford University Press, 2007. Ch. 26, '"Down in the terraces between the targets': Civilians", Peter Robinson, contains commentary on 'The Entertainment of War' and 'Wonders of Obligation', pp. 520–522.

Pinko Scum Psychotope, Andrew Duncan's website, contains a section on Roy Fisher. Go to: www.pinko.org/58.html: you will need to scroll down the page. This section also appears, very slightly revised, in Duncan's book, *Origins of the Underground* (see below).

Origins of the Underground: British Poetry between Apocryphon and Incident Light 1933–79, Andrew Duncan. Cambridge, Salt Publishing, 2008. 'Birmingham Engulfed by Pattern: Roy Fisher', pp.62–70.

The Powys Journal, Vol. 18, 2008, pp. 9–29. Charles Lock: 'Reading a Dedication: Roy Fisher and John Cowper Powys.'

A Concise Companion to Postwar British and Irish Poetry, ed. Nigel Alderton and C.D. Blanton, Chichester, Wiley-Blackwell, 2009. Ch.4,

a bibliography

'Region and Nation in Britain and Ireland', Michael Thurston, pp.88–91 and Ch.10, 'Place, Space, and Landscape', Eric Falci, pp.209–212 and pp.216–219, contain commentary on RF.

An Unofficial Roy Fisher, ed. Peter Robinson. Exeter, Shearsman Books, 2010. Contains poems and/or prose connected with RF by Fleur Adcock, Ann Atkinson, Eleanor Cooke, Kelvin Corcoran, Peter Didsbury, Laurie Duggan, Georgina Hammick, Peter Hughes, August Kleinzahler, R. F. Langley, Angela Leighton, Charles Lock, Peter Makin, John Matthias, Ian McMillan, Peter Middleton, Michael O'Neill, Tom Pickard, Ralph Pite, Ian Pople, Richard Price, Peter Riley, Peter Robinson, Robert Sheppard, Matthew Sperling, Jeffrey Wainwright, John Welch, David Wheatley, and John Wilkinson.

H. Readings on Film/DVD

Word of Mouth 1 (1990): The first of a ten-part series produced for Border Television in which poets read their work. RF reads 'The Entertainment of War'. Further details are available at http://artsonfilm.wmin.ac.uk/films.php?a=view&recid=211

Powys Society Conference, 2007. DVD. RF reads 'The Poetry Promise', 'Masterpieces in My Sleep', 'Staffordshire Red', from 'A Furnace' (from Section II, 'The Return'), 'Of the Empirical Self and for Me', and 'The Home Pianist's Companion'.

I. Translations by Roy Fisher

Modern Poetry in Translation: 20, 2002. Two poems by Mariya Kildibekova: 'Pizza's a populous island' and 'Everybody was going on talking the same talk.' This issue is available on-line at http://www.poetrymagazines.org.uk/magazine/issue.asp?id=462 The translations can also be found in *An Anthology of Contemporary Russian Women Poets*, ed. Valentina Polukhina and Daniel Weissbort (Iowa: University of Iowa Press, 2005 and also Manchester: Carcanet Press, 2005).

notes on contributors

Notes on Contributors

Fleur Adcock was born in New Zealand but has lived in England since 1963. Her previous collections of poetry, now out of print, have been replaced by *Poems 1960–2000* (Tarset: Bloodaxe Books, 2000) and a new collection, *Dragon Talk*, appearing in 2010. She has also published translations from Romanian and Medieval Latin poetry, and edited several anthologies, including *The Faber Book of 20th Century Women's Poetry*. In 2006 she was awarded the Queen's Gold Medal for Poetry.

Ann Atkinson co-edited *Staple* for seven years and is currently Derbyshire's Poet Laureate. Her pamphlet, *Drawing Water*, is published by Smith Doorstop.

Eleanor Cooke has published several books of poetry including *Secret Files* (Jonathan Cape) and *Who Killed Prees Heath?* (Bristol Classical Press and SWT). A new collection is forthcoming from Salt. She has lectured in creative writing and contemporary literature, taken part in the Writers in Schools scheme, written three plays for the stage, and programmes for Radio 4.

Kelvin Corcoran's first book *Robin Hood in the Dark Ages* (1985) was followed by eight subsequent collections. *New and Selected Poems* is available from Shearsman Books. The sequence *Helen Mania* was made a Poetry Book Society Choice in 2005. An interview is included in *Don't Start Me Talking* (Salt, 2007). *Backward Turning Sea*, published by Shearsman in 2008, includes an extended sequence on the work of the painter Roger Hilton. *Not the Full Story*, six interviews with the poet Lee Harwood, also appeared from Shearsman in 2008. Longbarrow Press published his recent work in 2009.

Peter Didsbury was born in 1946, in Fleetwood, Lancashire. His published poetry collections, all from Bloodaxe Books, include: *The Butchers of Hull* (1982), *The Classical Farm* (1987), and *That Old-Time Religion* (1994). The two latter collections were Poetry Book Society Recommendations. His fourth full-length collection, *A Natural History*, is included in *Scenes from a Long Sleep: New & Collected Poems* (2003). He received a Cholmondely Award in 1989. He works as a consultant archaeologist in Hull, and is a Fellow of the Society of Antiquaries.

Laurie Duggan was born in Melbourne and currently lives in Faversham, Kent. Recent poetry books are *Crab & Winkle* (Exeter: Shearsman Books, 2009), *Compared to What: Selected Poems 1971–2003*, (Shearsman, 2005)

notes on contributors

and *The Passenger*, (Brisbane: University of Queensland Press, 2006). He is also the author of *Ghost Nation: Imagined Space and Australian Visual Culture, 1901–1939* (UQP, 2001). His blog, *Graveney Marsh*, is online at www.graveneymarsh.blogspot.com.

Roy Fisher, who provides the occasion for, and is the subject of, this collection, was born on 11 June 1930 in Handsworth, Birmingham. He won a scholarship to the local grammar school, and later secured a place at Birmingham University where he read English and first published poems in the student magazine. To earn a living and support a family, he went into teaching, first at a grammar school in Newton Abbott, Devon, in the 1950s; he then returned to Birmingham and a job in a college of education. He was principal lecturer and head of department of English and Drama at Bordesley College of Education in Birmingham from 1963 to 1971, when he became a member of the Department of American Studies at Keele University. Through these three decades he pursued a second career as a semi-professional jazz musician. Since retiring he has lived in the Peak District. His early pamphlets, including *City* (1961) and *Ten Interiors with Various Figures* (1966) were first brought together in *Collected Poems 1968*. A larger gathering of further books and pamphlets, such as *The Ship's Orchestra* (1966), *Matrix* (1971), some of *The Cut Pages* (1971) and *The Thing about Joe Sullivan* (1978), appeared from OUP as *Poems 1955–1980* (enlarged paperback edition, *Poems 1955–1987*). The long poem *A Furnace* also appeared from OUP in 1986, as did *Birmingham River* (1994). In 1996, Bloodaxe Books published *The Dow Low Drop: New and Selected Poems*. Bloodaxe now publish *The Long and the Short of It: Poems 1955–2005* and *Standard Midland* (2010). Fisher's *Interviews Through Time and Selected Prose* (2000) is available from Shearsman Books.

Georgina Hammick has published two novels, and two volumes of short stories. She is working on a third collection.

Peter Hughes lives on the Norfolk coast. His recent poetry collections, *Nistanimera* (2006) and *The Summer of Agios Dimitrios* (2009), were both published by Shearsman. *Blueroads: Selected Poems* came out from Salt in 2003. Peter runs Oystercatcher Press, winner of the 2009 Michael Marks award for outstanding publisher of poetry in pamphlet form: www.oystercatcherpress.com.

Siân Hughes has been a Roy Fisher fan since 1983, and the best parts of her brain operate something like a tribute band, but it's probably coincidence that she spent two years living in Birmingham in the 1980s trying to write prose poetry. Her collection *The Missing* (Salt, 2009) was a PBS Recommendation, and was short-listed for the Forward, Aldeburgh and Guardian first book awards.

Ronald King was born in Brazil in 1932 and came to England at the age of 12. In 1967 he formed Circle Press to 'draw together a circle of like-minded people' to design, print and distribute Artists Books. Since then he has collaborated with more than 100 artists, writers, and poets, including 9 projects with Roy Fisher. He lives with his wife, the sculptor Willow Legge, in West Sussex.

August Kleinzahler's most recent book is *Music: I–LXXIV*, a collection of music essays from Pressed Wafer Press. He lives in San Francisco.

R.F. Langley's books include *Collected Poems* (Manchester: Carcanet/ infernal methods, 2000), *Journals* (Exeter: Shearsman Books, 2006), and *The Face of It* (Carcanet, 2007).

Angela Leighton is the author of two volumes of poetry, *A Cold Spell* (2000) and *Sea Level* (2007), both with Shoestring, as well as various works of criticism, most recently *On Form: Poetry, Aestheticism, and the Legacy of a Word* (OUP, 2007), which includes a chapter about Roy Fisher. She is Senior Research Fellow at Trinity College, Cambridge.

Charles Lock is the author of 'Reading a Dedication: Roy Fisher and John Cowper Powys' (2008). Formerly at the University of Toronto, he has been Professor of English Literature at the University of Copenhagen since 1996, and has also published on Anne Blonstein, Geoffrey Hill, Les Murray and Derek Walcott.

Peter Makin's publications include *Pound's Cantos* (Baltimore: Johns Hopkins UP, 1992), *Bunting: The Shaping of His Verse* (Oxford: Clarendon Press, 1992), (ed.) *Basil Bunting on Poetry* (Baltimore: Johns Hopkins University Press, 1999) and (ed.) *Ezra Pound's Cantos: A Casebook* (Oxford: OUP, 2006). He lives in a village in Kyoto Prefecture.

John Matthias taught for many years at the University of Notre Dame and still edits *Notre Dame Review*. He has published some twenty-five books of poetry, translation, criticism, and collaboration. His most recent books of poetry are *Kedging* (2007), a bilingual selected poems, *Nuotando a*

notes on contributors

mezzanotte (2008), published in Italy with translations by Gabriele Poole, and *Trigons* (Exeter: Shearsman Books, 2010).

Ian McMillan was born in 1956 and he's been a Roy Fisher fan since 1980 and a freelance writer, performer and broadcaster since 1981. He's currently presenting *The Verb* on Radio 3, touring with The Ian McMillan Orchestra, and collaborating with photographers and visual artists on books and exhibition projects, inspired by Roy Fisher's example of mixing genres with joy and delight.

Peter Middleton is the author of *Aftermath* (Cambridge: Salt Publishing, 2003), and several books on modern literature including *Distant Reading* (2005), essays mainly about poetry and performance.

Michael O'Neill is a Professor of English and a Director of the Institute of Advanced Study at Durham University. His recent critical books include *The All-Sustaining Air: Romantic Legacies and Renewals in British, American, and Irish Poetry since 1900* (OUP, 2007). His second collection of poems, *Wheel*, was published by Arc in 2008.

Tom Pickard's last three books of poems, *Hole in the Wall*, *The Dark Months of May*, and *Ballad of Jamie Allan* are published by Flood Editions, Chicago. The last became a finalist in the National Book Critics Circle awards. *Ballad of Jamie Allan* was also a libretto for a 'folk opera' composed by John Harle, commissioned by the Sage Gateshead for their opening season. Pickard recently collaborated with Harle on a piece for saxophone, organ and chorus to celebrate the 500th anniversary of London Bridge, performed in 2009 at Southwark Cathedral by Harle on saxophone and sung by Cambridge's Kings College Choir. In 1991 he produced and directed a 50-minute film on Roy Fisher, *Birmingham's What I Think With*. He lives in the North Pennines.

Ralph Pite teaches English at the University of Bristol. He has written on Romanticism, modern poetry and Thomas Hardy, including a biography, *Thomas Hardy: The Guarded Life* (London: Picador, 2006). He is currently working on a study of Robert Frost and Edward Thomas. A book of his poems, *Paths and Ladders*, came out from the Brodie Press, Bristol, in 2003.

Ian Pople's *An Occasional Lean-to* (2005) is published by Arc Publications, Todmorden.

Richard Price is a poet, novelist and curator. His collections include *Lucky Day* (Manchester: Carcanet, 2005), shortlisted for the Whitbread Poetry Prize, *Rays* (Carcanet, 2009), a book of love poems, and two collaborations with the book artist Ronald King, *gift horse* and *little but often*. His novel *The Island*, published in 2010, has been described by Toby Litt as 'one of the most beautiful nightmares you'll ever have.' As Head of Modern British Collections at the British Library, he has curated exhibitions including *Migrant the Magnificent* and *Ted Hughes: The Page is Printed*.

Tom Raworth remembers the pleasure of Fulcrum's *The Ship's Orchestra* and of hearing Roy play (even one-handed). After a year of wandering, he lives in Hove where he occasionally writes and makes images but more frequently looks at the sea.

Peter Riley was born in Stockport in 1940. He has had fifteen books published, mostly of poetry, the latest a book of prose poems, *Greek Passages* (Exeter: Shearsman Books, 2009). In 1985 he returned to Cambridge after a varied lack of career, and ran a poetry book business until he retired in 2005.

Peter Robinson's most recent collection is *The Look of Goodbye: Poems 2001–2006* (2008) from Shearsman, who also publish *Spirits of the Stair: Selected Aphorisms* (2009). Among other recent books are *Poetry & Translation: The Art of the Impossible* (Liverpool University Press, 2010) and *The Greener Meadow: Selected Poems of Luciano Erba* (Princeton University Press, 2007), awarded the John Florio Prize. *English Nettles and Other Poems*, a limited edition with artworks by Sally Castle, is just out from Two Rivers Press.

Robert Sheppard co-edited *News for the Ear*, a previous homage to Roy Fisher and he has written about his work in *The Poetry of Saying: British Poetry and Its Discontents 1950–2000* (Liverpool University Press, 2005) and elsewhere. He has published a couple of previous poems dedicated to Fisher in *Complete Twentieth Century Blues*, his long poetic project published by Salt in 2008. Shearsman publish his *Warrant Error*. He is Professor of Poetry and Poetics at Edge Hill University, and is the editor of the *Journal for British and Irish Innovative Poetry*.

Derek Slade is, after more than thirty years as a teacher in Further Education, thoroughly enjoying his retirement.

notes on contributors

Matthew Sperling teaches Modern English Literature at Keble College, Oxford. His essay on Roy Fisher's collaborations with book-artist Ronald King at the Circle Press appeared in the Modern Book History number of the journal *Literature Compass* vol. 4 (July 2007).

Sue Stanford, born 1937, arrived at Bordesley College from London as Sue Birch. She has recently retired as Chair of Governors of Yale College, Wrexham. Her friendship with Roy Fisher and his family has continued to this day.

Ian Tyson, a printmaker and book artist, was born in Wallasey, Cheshire, England, in 1933, and studied at the Birkenhead School of Art. He taught drawing and printmaking at various colleges of art and has been a visiting professor at the Royal College of Art (1984), the University of Wisconsin, Madison (1969), at the University of California, San Diego (1992), and a Brinkley Fellow at the Norwich School of Art (1979–1980). He has had over fourteen solo and thirty group exhibitions throughout Europe. He ran the Tetrad Press for many years and collaborated with Roy Fisher.

Jeffrey Wainwright's most recent poetry collection is *Clarity or Death!* (Manchester: Carcanet Press, 2008). His previous volume was *Out of the Air* (Carcanet, 1999). He is also the author of *Poetry the Basics* (London: Routledge, 2004) and *Acceptable Words: Essays on the Poetry of Geoffrey Hill* (Manchester University Press, 2006).

John Welch was born in London in 1942. In 1975 he founded the Many Press, publishing much new poetry over the next thirty years or so. Shearsman Books published his *Collected Poems* in 2007, and his latest collection, *Visiting Exile*, in 2009.

David Wheatley is the author of three collections of poetry with Gallery Press: *Thirst* (1997), *Misery Hill* (2000), and *Mocker* (2006). He lectures at the University of Hull and recently edited the *Selected Poems* of Samuel Beckett for Faber & Faber.

John Wilkinson is an English poet now teaching at the University of Notre Dame, Indiana. He lived in Birmingham and in Dudley from 1980 to 1994, working in various mental health facilities in Handsworth, Rubery, Solihull, Walsall, Newtown, and Acocks Green. His recent books of poetry include *Lake Shore Drive* (2006) and *Down to Earth* (2008) both from Salt Publishing.

'John Cage played one piece that consisted of four and a half minutes of silence in his 1980 performance of avant garde music.'

(Photograph and caption from Archives, The Dome, *University of Notre Dame, Indiana, USA.)*

www.ingramcontent.com/pod-product-compliance
Lightning Source LLC
Chambersburg PA
CBHW032251150426
43195CB00008BA/415